MODEL TRAINS

RAILROADS IN THE MAKING

With an introduction by Gerald Pollinger

CRESCENT BOOKS

Contents

All illustrations in this volume were photographed by Carlo Bevilacqua

Based on the Italian by Uberto Tosco

Printed in Italy by IGDA, Novara
Library of Congress Catalog Card No: 72-84331

The world of model railways extends far beyond the confines of the toyshop window and children's playroom; it reaches into the homes of countless people, of every age and occupation, enthusiasts who devote much of their lives to recreating – albeit on a small scale – one of science's greatest achievements. Their enthusiasm is not misplaced: train modelling is neither a childish pursuit nor a mindless escape from the everyday world, but a hobby that calls for both resourcefulness and creativity.

This book, with its magnificent full-colour illustrations of some of the world's best proprietary models, is intended to provide further incentives for the dedicated train modeller, and at the same time show the as-yet uncommitted what high standards of craftsmanship are achieved in this absorbing field. The introductory text is addressed primarily to the novice: from a brief survey of the history of the industry, it passes to explanations of the technical details involved, notably choice of gauge, scale, power and trackwork, and then gives pointers to those seeking advice on the control and planning of a layout. At the same time, the more experienced model train enthusiasts will find an important comprehensive list of all the gauges and scales commonly in use, as well as a discussion of different types of equipment and loco classification.

The colour plates that follow not only provide examples of these classes, but also illustrate the variety of contributions made by different companies all over the world to the model industry, and in particular show the increasing accuracy and realism of its products. We hope that this book will draw new, talented recruits into the ranks of train modellers and demonstrate that here is a hobby that can fascinate and reward the enthusiast for a lifetime.

The growth of an industry

Models of railways and of trains are as old as the railways and trains themselves: a few fortunate collectors of the earliest models can point with pride to items that appeared in England in the 1830s, just ten years after the opening of the first stretch of the Stockton and Darlington line, whose first steam locomotive, 'Locomotion No. 1' took the rails on 27 September 1825.

Models of proposed locomotives and rolling stock had in fact been made before this date, and certainly a citizen of Prague, one von Gerstner, was using models for demonstration purposes as early as 1813. About this time also, British designers were visiting the United States of America with models of locomotives, while American engineers visiting Britain took home with them models of trains for the use of the early American railroad companies. Models such as these were, of course, fairly large, and the first miniature model trains as we know them today did not appear until about halfway through the nineteenth century. These were manufactured in England, in France, and in Germany, and were steam locomotives, principally made of brass. They were followed by tin locomotives made in America, and, at the end of the century, by wooden pull-along trains.

Prominent among the earliest manufacturers were two companies who still carry on the tradition: Märklin of Goppingen, Germany, and Lionel of New York, founded in 1859 and 1900 respectively. A number of other famous manufacturers came into the field in the early part of the twentieth century, including the British firm Meccano in 1915 (to become Hornby Trains in 1921), which had been preceded by Bassett-Lowke in 1892, and also Bing in Germany (from 1865 till 1933), and these were later joined by Fleischmann. In America the pioneers were Ives with Beggs, followed by Marx, American Flyer, and Auburn.

Most of the early miniature rails were of larger dimensions than they are today. During the first half of this century the most popular gauge (the distance between the two running rails), was $2\frac{7}{8}$ inches, although other gauges, notably $2\frac{1}{8}$ inches, $1\frac{3}{4}$ inches and later $1\frac{1}{4}$ inches, were also in use. The first very small trains suitable for table-top use were made in 1920 by Bing in Germany, with a gauge of only $\frac{5}{8}$ inches, and a year later these were introduced into England by the late W. J. Bassett-Lowke. Hornby and Lionel did not start manufacturing these little models until 1938, and in the meanwhile Trix and Fleischmann had produced quite a number of such models in Germany. (An even smaller practical gauge of 0.471 inches was introduced by the American company Harold Products about 1960, and this did become popular in Britain, although it has recently been superseded by a much smaller gauge, for which the track and models were originally zinc alloy toys.)

In order to obtain a certain amount of order and co-operation between manufacturers of model railway equipment, certain organizations have been formed which lay down recommended standards. These include the National Model Railroad Association of America, the British Railway Modelling Standards Bureau, and the Normes Européennes Modelfer (NEM) in Europe. Unfortunately these organizations have not always had all the support that they deserve, with a result that there remains – particularly in Britain – a confusion in standards that serves only to make the life of the modeller who wishes to work to scale standards somewhat difficult.

Model railroads and toy trains are two quite separate things, and the day is rapidly approaching when, as a result of both important new manufacturing processes and higher standards, the toy train of yesterday will become the miniature scale model of tomorrow, reproducing every feature of the prototype in exact detail.

The illustrations that appear in this book are primarily of Italian and German models, for the book originally appeared in Italy. In nearly every case they show a high standard of accuracy and attention to detail, for the European model railway manufacturers whose work is photographed in these pages have long made realism their aim, and their craft is shown pictorially to great effect. Indeed, when one can purchase ready-to-run models, or

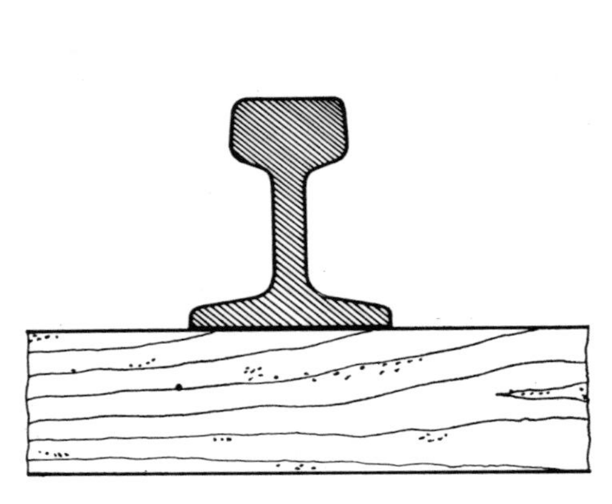

All model rail is allocated code numbers, which refer to the basic dimensions of the rail. The most important of these are the overall height, the width of the base, and the width and depth of the head. This drawing shows flat bottom rail in profile.

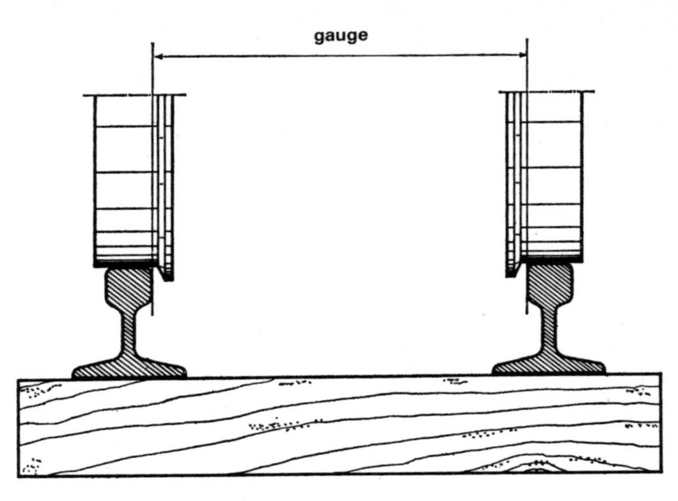

A diagram of the train wheels, as they sit on the rail. The width of the tread on the rail, the overall width of the tire, the depth and width of the flange, and the back-to-back measurement are all important for easy running and interchange.

construction kits of models like these, there seems little point in buying a 'toy train', and having second best.

Gauge and scale

To a novice modeller, two of the most confusing terms are *gauge* and *scale*, and this confusion is enhanced by the fact that these words are often used incorrectly – not least by some manufacturers, who are often guilty, for example, of indicating that HO and OO gauges are the same thing – which is in fact not the case, for each uses a different scale.

Quite simply, the gauge is the distance between the two running rails. In prototype railways this is generally expressed in feet and inches or metres, and in model railways in inches and fractions (particularly with the larger gauges), or in millimetres.

The majority of the world's railways use the Standard Gauge of 4 feet 8½ inches, and this is the one on which most model railways are based. However, there are many other gauges in use in many countries, and these have also been made use of by the modellers. These include the metre gauge (3 feet 3⅜ inches), used in Brazil and Burma, and those of 5 feet 6 inches in India and Argentina, 5 feet 0 inches in Russia, 3 feet 0 inches in Colombia, and 1 foot 11⅝ inches in Peru.

But whatever gauge is used for a model, it is related to the scale, which quite simply substitutes one unit of measurement for one unit of measurement on the original. Thus, on a prototype one foot equals one foot, and if a half-scale model were made of this prototype, six inches on the model would equal one foot on the original. Gauges and scales have been awarded symbols: for example, in the most widely used, the HO gauge, the distance between the running rails is 16.5 millimetres, representing 4 feet 8½ inches, reduced in proportion to the scale of the rolling stock used upon it, to a scale of 3.5 millimetres to the foot. The table on pages 7 and 8 gives a similar detailed survey of the other gauges and scales to be found in use in model railways all over the world at the present time, tabulated in descending order of size.

Most of the models in the illustrations in this book are for HO gauge, with a scale of 3.5 millimetres to the foot, but there are also some British models included that run on the same gauge of 16.5 millimetres, but are built to the oversize scale of 4 millimetres to the foot.

In addition to these models, there are also models of trains for narrow gauges, that is, less than the standard gauge of 4 feet 8½ inches. Normally one does not model the larger gauges of 3 feet 6 inches and one metre that are in prototype use all over the world, but there are many models of the 3 feet, 2 feet 6 inches, 2 feet 3 inches and 2 feet gauges. The table on page 9 summarizes the most common narrow gauges in use.

With the introduction of the Z gauge of 6.5 millimetres, it will be possible to model narrow gauges in other scales, using 4 millimetre scale models to represent the 18 inch gauge prototype that is often used for public miniature railways, using a scale of 4¾ inches to the foot.

Power and trackwork

This book deals principally with model trains that run on a track gauge of 16.5 millimetres and are built to a scale of either 3.5 or 4 millimetres to the foot. We will ignore two of the forms of propulsion, steam (although it has been used) and the hand (which is always in use!), and concentrate solely on trains powered by clockwork or electric current.

Bing Brothers of Nuremberg were one of the earliest producers of OO gauge trains, between the years 1924 and 1926. The most common locomotive was a 2–4–0T tank engine, powered by clockwork or by a 4–6 volt accumulator (as liquid batteries were then known). The track was metal based with two rails for clockwork trains, and included a third insulated central rail for electric trains.

In England, Bassett-Lowke of Northampton had produced much the same trains as Bing before the Depression of 1926, and in 1935 introduced the Trix-Twin

Gauges and scales

NAME	GAUGE	DESCRIPTION
3	$2\frac{1}{2}$ ins (63.50 mm)	In 1902 the first commercial models appeared with this gauge. Three scales are used: $\frac{1}{2}$ in, $\frac{17}{32}$ in, or 14 mm to the foot
STANDARD	$2\frac{1}{8}$ ins (53.97 mm)	Much in vogue before 1938, this American gauge used a scale of $\frac{3}{8}$ in to the foot, or sometimes $\frac{7}{16}$ in.
2	2 ins (50.97 mm)	Not much used. The scale used was normally $\frac{7}{16}$ in to the foot, and the scale ratio was 1:26 or 1:27.
1F	45 mm	A fine scale version of a gauge ideal for use in garden railways. The scale is 10 mm to the foot. The ratio is 1:30.5.
1	$1\frac{3}{4}$ ins (44.45 mm)	Britain uses a scale of 10 mm to the foot; Germany and the USA have a scale of $\frac{3}{8}$ ins and a scale ratio of 1:32.
O_{17}	$1\frac{1}{4}$ ins (31.75 mm)	Using English instead of metric measurements, this rarely used gauge uses a scale of $\frac{17}{64}$ ins to the foot.
O	32 mm	Appearing before the First World War, the British O Gauge is still popular. The scale is 7 mm to the foot.
OF	32 mm	Also with a scale of 7 mm to the foot, this gauge uses much finer measurements; the rail height, for example, is only half that of O. Ratio: 1:43.5.
O	$1\frac{1}{4}$ ins	In America a scale of $\frac{1}{4}$ in to the foot is normal, and a ratio of 1:48, as opposed to the 1:45.2 ratio of O_{17}.
O	$1\frac{1}{8}$ ins	A number of Continental models have appeared using this gauge, built to a scale of 2 cm to 1 metre.
Q	$1\frac{3}{16}$ ins	Also referred to as a gauge of 1.188 in, this American gauge uses a scale of $\frac{1}{4}$ in to the foot. It has been replaced by O.
HI	$\frac{7}{8}$ ins	Literally half of Gauge 1, this gauge was superseded by S Gauge. It has a scale of $\frac{3}{15}$ ins to the foot.
S	$\frac{7}{8}$ ins	Quite common in the USA, with a scale of $\frac{3}{16}$ ins to the foot and a ratio of 1:64; Europe prefers to express the gauge as 22.2 mm and the ratio as 1:65.
OO	$\frac{3}{4}$ ins (19 mm)	Much confusion derives from the use by America of a 19 mm gauge with a scale of 4 mm to the foot and a ratio of 1:76.2.
EEM	18.83 mm	Originally called EMF Gauge, this was a British fine scale attempt, superseded by the Protofour group, using a scale of 4 mm/1 ft and a 1:76.2 ratio.
EM	18 mm	Since the gauge/scale relationship of the British OO Gauge is inaccurate, quite a number of modellers use 18 mm as a gauge with a 4 mm scale.
OO	16.5 mm	The most common British gauge, with a scale of 4 mm to the foot (giving a top-heavy overscale appearance but useful for including large motors in small locos).
HO	16.5 mm	The most widely used gauge. The scale is normally 3.5 mm to the foot and the ratio 1:87.1. Some models have used a 3.8 mm scale.
OOE	16.5	There are still a number of French and German models using this gauge with a scale of 1 cm to the metre, and a scale ratio of 1:91.
HOE	16 mm	Rarely used, this gauge was replaced by HO Gauge. It had a scale of 3.5 mm to the foot.
E	$\frac{19}{32}$ ins	Another rare gauge, also replaced by HO gauge with a scale of $\frac{1}{8}$ in to the foot. The gauge is also called 15 mm.

NAME	GAUGE	DESCRIPTION
QO	0.6 ins	This is a very rare American gauge, in which the models are built to a scale of $\frac{1}{8}$ in to the foot.
OOC	14.3 mm	This Continental scale aims to obtain a perfect scale ratio of 1:100 with a scale of 1 cm to 1 metre.
TM	13.5 mm	A British fine scale/gauge ratio of TT Gauge, using the standard British scale of 3 mm to the foot.
TT–3	12 mm	The commonly used British table-top gauge with a scale of 3 mm to the foot, giving an oversized effect. The ratio is 1:101.6.
TT	12 mm	The original table-top gauge of 0.471 in, with a scale of 2.5 mm (European) or $\frac{1}{10}$ in (USA) to the foot, and a ratio of 1:120.
TT–X	12 mm	A few British modellers decided to scale down the British TT–3 Gauge, and use a scale of $\frac{1}{9}$ in to the foot.
HOO	10 mm	Known as *centimetrico*, or micro-gauge. It is in use in Sweden, with a scale of 2 mm to the foot and a ratio of 1:144.
OOO	9.5 mm	Fifty years ago the first models appeared for this gauge. The scale is 2 mm to the foot and there is an active Scale Association. Ratio: 1:152.4.
N	9 mm	The British modeller uses a scale of 2.06 mm to the foot, which is a ratio of 1:148, and gives a slightly overscale effect.
N	9 mm	On the Continent of Europe, the ratio used to be 1:150, but in 1960 was standardized at 1:160, with a scale of 1.9 mm to the foot.
K	8 mm	Only in Europe are there models to this small gauge, with a scale of 1.75 mm to the foot and a ratio of 1:180.
QOO	7.62 mm	Rarely used, except for special purposes at exhibitions, this is an American gauge with a scale of 1.75 mm to the foot.
Z	6.5 mm	Introduced in Germany in 1972, this minute gauge is likely to be the smallest commercially. The ratio is 1:220 and the scale 1.51 mm to the foot.
X	$\frac{3}{16}$ ins (4.5 mm)	In 1935 Mr Reg Walkley produced a scale model of an 0–4–0T tank locomotive to a scale of 1 mm to the foot. It operated perfectly.

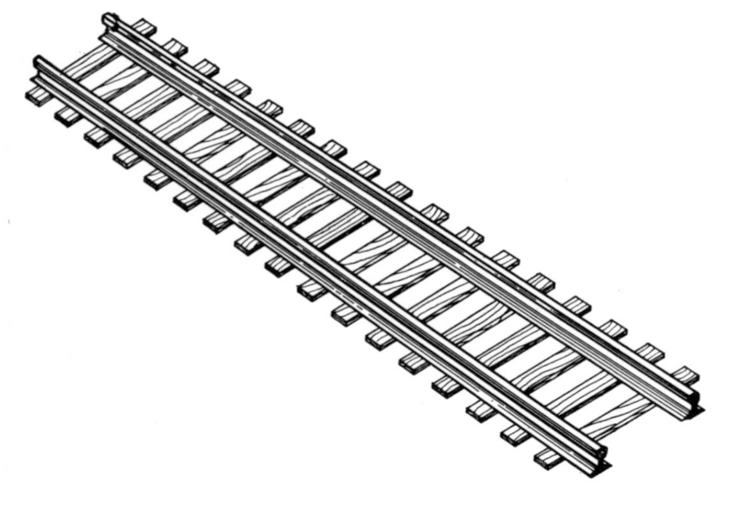

A level straight track is the only condition for the unhampered passage of wheels with flanges built to run on the same gauge. Complications start at curves, or where one rail crosses another, and to avoid derailments at such points the measurements of the trackwork must fit exactly those of the wheels of the model.

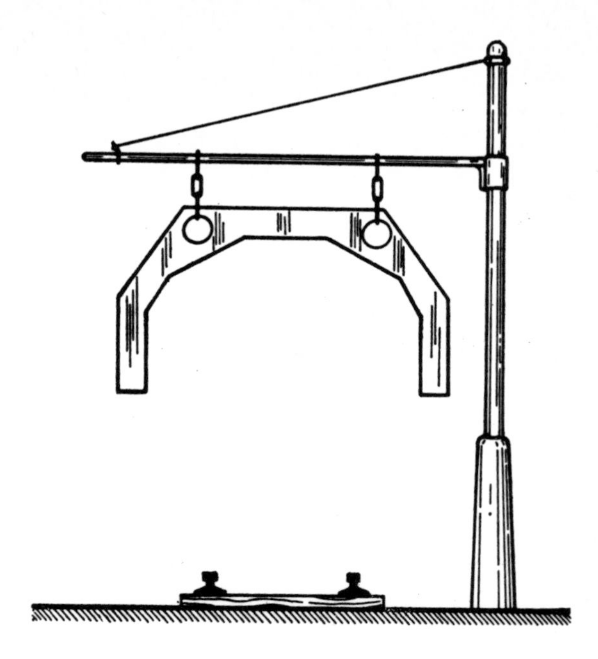

A loading gauge. This sets the limit on the height of a train so that it is able to pass safely under bridges and tunnels.

Narrow gauges

NAME	GAUGE	DESCRIPTION
Gm	45 mm	LBM are huge German models. Using Gauge 1 track, the scale is 22.5 mm to the foot.
O*n*	32 mm	Rolling stock for $2\frac{7}{8}$ ins Gauge, Gauge 3 and Gauge 1 use scales of 16 mm, 14 mm, and 10 mm to the foot representing 2 ft, 2 ft 3 ins and 3 ft prototypes.
O*n*3	19 mm	One of the three standard American narrow gauge models, with a scale of $\frac{1}{4}$ inch to the foot and a ratio of 1:48.
O*n*$2\frac{1}{2}$	16.5 mm	The scale used is $\frac{1}{4}$ in to the foot, and this enables HO items to be used to represent both 2 ft 3 ins and 2 ft 6 ins prototypes.
OO*n*	16.5 mm	Using 7 mm scale models – that is, those normally built for Gauge O – on trackwork half the size will represent 2 ft 3 ins and 2 ft 6 ins prototypes.
O*n*2	$\frac{1}{2}$ in	The second standard American narrow gauge uses $\frac{1}{4}$ inch scale models, and has a ratio of 1:48.
TT3*n*	12 mm	One British manufacturer makes models of Welsh narrow gauge railway locomotives and cars to a scale of $5\frac{1}{2}$ mm to the foot.
OO*n*3	12 mm	To represent a 3 ft gauge prototype, one British manufacturer issues Isle of Man models to a scale of 4 mm to the foot.
TT*n*	12 mm	An East German company markets a number of models of German and Austrian equipment to a scale of 3.5 mm to the foot.
HO*n*3	10.5 mm	On 0.413 inch gauge, many Americans model to a scale of 3.5 mm and a ratio of 1:87.1 to represent 3 ft gauge prototypes.
OO9	9 mm	Strictly speaking, this is OO*n*2.25 Gauge, using a scale of 4 mm to the foot to represent 2 ft 3 in prototypes.
HO*n*$2\frac{1}{2}$	9 mm	The smallest scale for narrow gauges in common use is 3.5 mm to the foot to represent 2 ft 6 in prototypes. It is also called HO*n*9.

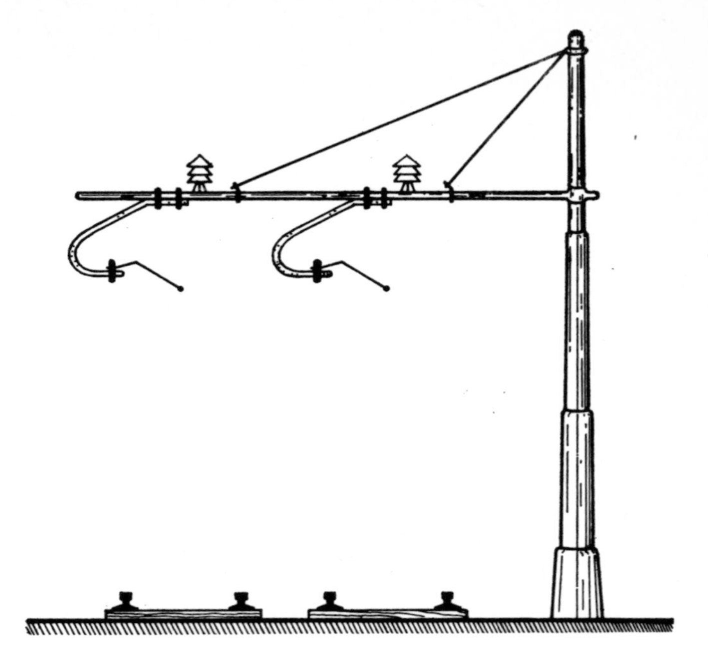

Right: A type of equipment for overhead pickup. There are suggested standards for overhead electric and traction power pickup, including not only the thickness of the wire rod, and its height above the head of the rail, but also by how much the wire can be offset from the centre of the track below.

range. Like Bing, this used a 16 millimetre gauge (described as OO), and the scale chosen by Henry Greenly of 4 millimetres to the foot gave a ratio of 1:80. The 'universal' motors operated on 12 volts DC (using an easy multiple of the 2 volts direct current accumulator – an interesting historical event in view of the future) or preferably 14 volts AC. Alternating current was used to reverse the motors, and later to operate remote uncoupling devices in the tender. The controller gave a continuous sequence of ahead, stop, reverse, stop, which was often unsatisfactory. The trackwork had a Bakelite base, $\frac{3}{8}$ inches high, with three running rails, each insulated from the base. This last feature gave the operator the unique possibility of having two engines working independently on one section of track: one loco had pick-up brushes for the current over the left-hand rail, the other had them on the right-hand rail, and both used the centre rail as a common return. Meanwhile, in Nuremberg, Trix Express continued its own separate development using a smaller scale of 3.5 millimetres.

In 1937, Hornby-Dublo produced its OO gauge trains in clockwork and electric versions, standardizing on 12 volts DC for operation. The products from the Liverpool factory were far in advance of anything that had so far appeared, and set the pattern for future scale developments: the trackwork was two-rail for clockwork, or three-rail for electric operation, the central third rail serving as the insulated rail, with pick-up working through brushes situated under the centre of the engines.

By 1939, OO gauge was beginning to make inroads on the O gauge fraternity in Europe, but in America little was done about HO gauge until 1940, and it was not until 1948 that the smaller scale started to become popular there. Then in 1950, Rovex introduced their OO gauge toy trains into England. Unlike the metal models of Hornby-Dublo, these were plastic, and much cheaper than the few Trix-Twin models that were available. They set as a standard the two-rail system, both rails being mounted on a plastic grey base, and thus insulated from each other.

Rovex became Tri-ang, then Tri-ang-Hornby when they subsequently absorbed Hornby-Dublo, but have continued to use the 12 volt DC two-rail system, although they have many times changed the type of track used. At present it is of tinned steel or nickel silver on a plastic base, which represents the wooden cross ties or sleepers.

To keep pace with their rivals, Trix Express, (as Bing was by now known), went over to 12 volts DC operation in 1956, shortly followed by Trix-Twin, both companies using fibre-based track with three insulated rails for the twin system. In 1963 Trix dispensed with their ugly shoes and used the wheels for pick-up, as is now commonplace, and in 1964 they introduced two-rail trackage, which was important in view of a tie-up with Liliput, who made two-rail locos and no three-rail type. By July 1970 Trix Trains had withdrawn all the three-rail Trix-Twin locomotives, and an era had ended.

It was left to Hornby-Dublo to introduce the two-rail system, using nickel silver rail on a plastic moulded base that incorporated the individual sleepers, giving us a track that is now the universal standard. But this was not until 1959, and although their superb locomotives live on under the auspices of Wrenn (who were themselves subsequently acquired by Tri-ang), the Hornby-Dublo trains as such are no more.

The German company Fleischmann was also early in the field with the two-rail system, which they had completely organized by 1956. They now have two parallel systems of trackwork which is some of the best in the world for operating and remote control facilities.

Others, namely the Italian Rivarossi of Como, later joined by Pocher of Turin, and the American company Atlas, started with a three-rail system operating on 15 volts AC, and a two-rail 12 volts DC system. They dropped the three-rail system in the early 1950s, but have developed and refined the two-rail trackwork for their smooth-running rolling stock.

Apart from Atlas, very little progress has been made in the American fields of snap-trackwork. As a result of the influence of the National Model Railroad

Association, a two-rail 12 volts DC system has been standardized, and in addition standards have been drawn up and agreed upon for just about every variable. In Europe, however, there is an astonishing number of different wheel dimensions (and also types of couplers, which will not mix). Thus, because of standardization, the American model railroader has been far ahead of enthusiasts in other countries, since about 1948, when HO gauge became popular. Far ahead, that is, in regard to kits, parts, and the supply of individual items, but not in the field of the toy train or the near-scale model train, for European manufacturers have tended to concentrate their energies on developing the 'train set', to which accessories can be added as and when desired.

Interchange, couplers and wheels

One loner remains: the German firm of Märklin have kept their original style of three-rail operation. Not until 1952 did they introduce their stud-contact system, which they improved in 1970. Although the third rail was taken away with the introduction of the stud-contact system, its place was taken by a series of studs sticking above the ties, contact being made by a shoe or skate under the loco. In addition to this, Märklin operate on an alternating current of up to 15 volts, with a 24 volt reversing circuit. This means that none of the other 16.5 millimetre gauge electric locos can be operated with Märklin equipment.

One other additional power source is overhead wires. There are a number of different catenary sections available for use with pantographs on top of the electric-type locomotives. One advantage of a catenary system is that is is possible to run two locos on one section of the track, one picking up from overhead and using one insulated rail for return current, while the other loco uses the two-rail system in the usual way.

To summarize, therefore: with the exception of Märklin, it should be possible to interchange all model railway rolling stock for 16.5 millimetre gauge. The only factors that might prevent this are the different types of coupler employed and the dimensions of the wheels, but it is perfectly possible to have one standard coupler on one's own layout. (The Peco type is already found on Trix Train, Trix-Twin, and Hornby-Dublo stock, and can be bought separately. The Tri-ang coupler is neat and unobtrusive, especially if the TT–3 gauge version is purchased for use with the larger trains, being similar to the American LaNal coupler.)

In America the National Model Railroad Association has recommended a contour shape to which all couplers should adhere to be compatible, and to look like the prototype, and in 1971 the German company Fleischmann introduced the 'Fox' coupler, which looks as though it may become a firm favourite with railway modellers. Whatever couplers are used, however, they must of course be mounted properly and at the same height, for otherwise automatic operation, if such is intended, will be impossible.

As for dimensions of wheels, the amount of tolerance available in the different sizes is very little. It is the dimensions of the wheels, combined with the dimensions of trackwork on a turnout, that makes for smooth, difficult, or impossible running.

The dimensions of a model wheel that have to be taken into account are the overall width of the tire, the width, depth and shape of the flange, the width of the tread, and the angle of the tread to the rail. In addition, there is the back-to-back measurement of the two wheels on their axle.

Obviously, if on an ordinary straight piece of track the back-to-back measurement is too wide, then one wheel will ride up on the rail, and if it is too narrow, the wheel will ride in the space between the rails.

The parts of a wheel are shown in the line drawings on page 15, and the different components of the piece of trackwork that is variously known as a point, a switch or a turnout on page 12. There are quite a few different types of point, but we are concerned here only with a straightforward left-hand turnout.

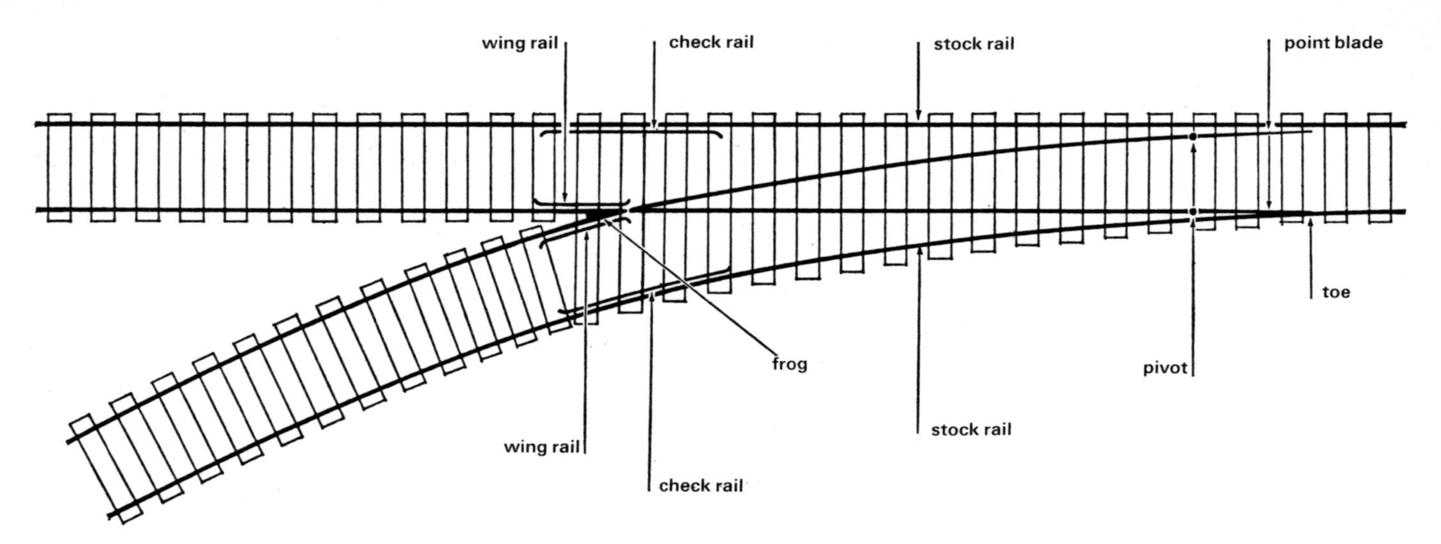

A drawing showing the parts of a point, also known as a turnout or a switch.

Some vital measurements

In order to avoid constant derailments, it is essential that the measurements of the trackwork where two rails cross each other marry with the wheels on your model. The gap between the frog and wing rail must not be too narrow, and must be deep enough to accommodate the flange. The radius of the curved closure rail must not be too sharp, and the check rails must be aligned properly.

If one is using, let us say, Fleischmann trains on Fleischmann track, there is no difficulty; but the use of Tri-ang stock on Hornby-Dublo points may create problems. Fortunately, however, wheels can be changed, and quite a few companies issue excellent scale wheels. One can also purchase scale track, which is often more realistic in operation and to look at than proprietary pieces.

The other 'vital statistics' with which we are concerned are the loading gauge, and the structure gauge. Obviously, a train must not be too high or too wide if it is to enter tunnels, negotiate platforms correctly, or pass other trains. If a model is built to scale, then all bridges, tunnels, and stations must be built to the same scale, and placed in relation to the model as they stood originally in relation to the prototype.

Realism and accuracy are what every modeller tries to strive for, sometimes without appreciating it; but true scale, or at least near-to-scale, models can be the source of an immense amount of satisfaction and pleasure to an enthusiast.

Control and planning

The proprietary manufacturers whose models appear in the colour plates in the second half of this book also make the electrical apparatus that controls the models, but there are also a number of electronic companies, including Codar, and Hammant and Morgan, who make power units specifically for model railways.

Generally speaking, 12 volt motors are used in model locomotives. These incorporate permanent magnets and require direct current. Basically, therefore, a control unit must consist of a transformer to convert the mains current of, for example, 110 volts or 240 volts alternating current into the 12 volts required, a rectifier to convert AC to DC, and a resistance or rheostat to control the amount of power transmitted.

As a result of the great advances in this field, there is no longer any need for bulky equipment, and one can purchase neat packs or units to mount in a control panel, for all the three accepted modern forms of controller. These are the variable voltage or the variable transformer, the earlier resistance controller, and the transistorized controller. Additional devices can be fitted to give extra slow running, various forms of braking or coasting, and remote control or lighting or uncoupling. One may also buy a complete sound pack that will emit any kind of whistle, screech, hiss, puff or clickety-clack noise, through a device in the loco or the tender.

There is no space here to discuss in detail the operation of model railways, the building of scenery, the laying of track upon a baseboard, and the finer forms of control. For information on these subjects the reader is recommended to study some of the many books that are readily available, but in particular to read one or more of the model railway magazines that are issued, generally monthly, in nearly every country of the world. The principal English language publications are two American periodicals, *Model Railroader* and *Railroad Model Craftsman*, and three British magazines, *Model Railways*, *Model Railway Constructor* and *Railway Modeller*. These in turn will lead you to the model railroad hobby shops, where any number of books for further reading and equipment may be purchased.

One of the more important topics discussed among railway modellers is that of layout planning. To start with it is a good idea to settle for one particular country for one's layout, and this choice is not always easy, for there are many types of model available, particularly of American, British, German, French, Scandinavian, Italian, and Swiss trains. Then when this choice has been made, a particular company should be selected, and here once again there is a very wide choice, although not all of the over 430 railroad companies in the USA have their counterpart in proprietary goods! The era may also be chosen, and both old-fashioned locos and the most modern new diesels are easy to come by.

Once country, company, and era are settled, thought should be given to the type of layout to be modelled. This may vary from a vast double mainline track with flyover junctions to a small single branch line in a standard or narrow gauge. The choice is entirely up to the owner, and the choice is wide. Again, lineside accessories for all the kinds of model railways may be bought in various forms, notably metal, castings, plastic and card or wood. The main point is that all these should be kept in proportion, in scale and – of course – in kind.

The types of trains operated should depend entirely on the purpose of the layout; real railways were not laid in an haphazard fashion, but were put down to serve a town or a port or an industry. Once one has decided upon the locale of the miniature railway train, formations can be made up to serve the points of interest, and thus locos and stock can be bought or made or assembled which will fit the scene like a glove. A layout will be more effective if it is inspired by a single idea, and if it is then carried through, right down to the choice of the smallest accessories.

Passenger and freight units

Many of the models illustrated in the pages that follow can be purchased in North America or Britain today, and can be used to form different kinds of train formations. The following are some possible units:

Express: For model expresses it is usual to have six or seven coaches hauled by powerful steam locos, of the Pacific Class or larger, or one or more diesels. Rolling stock can include dining cars, passenger cars, and perhaps vista-dome or observation cars. If you prefer large steam locos and have not much space, it is as well to remember that many 4–6–2 locos ended their journeys on long hauls pulling only a couple of coaches, having dropped or slipped others en route.

Night expresses: Four or five sleeping cars, hauled by a large loco or diesel unit, are the most usual. There are excellent models of both British and Continental Wagons-Lits on the market.

Main-line trains: Space decrees that fifteen-coach trains are difficult; the odd thing is that in miniature they do not look real. Four or five cars with, perhaps, a buffet car and certainly a baggage car or a brake-composite make a good combination. Multiple unit electric trains or diesel units are quite commonly used for these trains.

Suburban traffic: This varies from country to country and from era to era. One can use a 2–6–4T tank engine and a couple of suburban non-corridor coaches, or a twin-unit diesel set, or an electric set, or electric locos with overhead pantographs pulling a few cars.

Local traffic: Again, many variations are feasible. Small tank locos, or a diesel railcar, or interurban units or trolley cars, or push-pull cars with a loco between are all commonly used.

Branch lines: Enthusiasts of early models often want to use four or six-wheel coaches hauled by baby tank locos, whereas others prefer to use the more up-to-date diesel railcar. Where only a small space is available, a branch line model is suggested.

Milk trains: Various types of milk tankers are in use, and four or five of these with a utility van and a brake van, and sometimes also a passenger car form a suitable unit.

Breakdown: A 'Big Hook' with its attendant flat cars and a

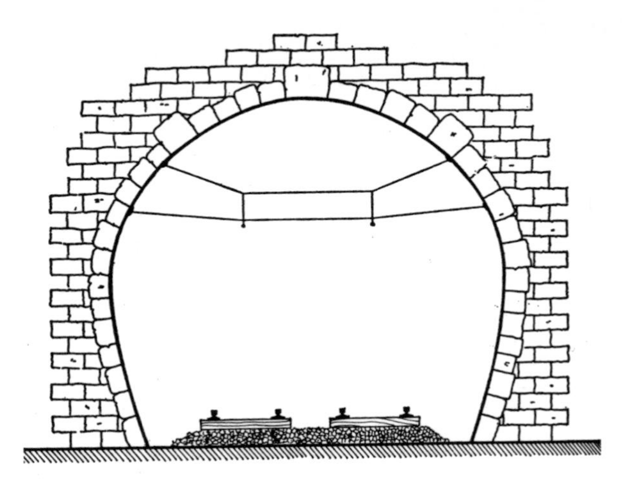

Right: Two diagrams showing typical contours for double track and single track tunnels, one containing overhead traction pickup wires.

brake van each end are necessary here, although a smaller version could make use of a crane truck. Track-laying trains also use the same set, and should include long flat cars to carry the rails.

Mail-trains: A Travelling Post Office car, with or without automatic pick-up apparatus is common, and several parcels cars can be incorporated as required. Note that 'Ocean Mails' cars are not used on mail trains, but on boat trains.

Boat trains: These generally consist of first class passenger cars and a couple of Pullman cars. Utility vans or 'Ocean Mails' cars make up this rake.

Pullman trains: Various countries run Pullmans in different colours. The different types of car can be made up into a rake of five or six; remember, however, that these cars are normally heavier than passenger coaches and a large loco unit may well be needed.

Additions: Many vacuum-brake fitted vehicles are run with passenger trains; these may include one or more milk tank wagons, parcels vans, baggage cars, utility vans, perishable fish or fruit vans, theatre scenery cars, and furniture container assemblies. It is up to the individual, of course, to select the additional pieces that he needs.

So far we have only mentioned varieties of passenger trains. Freight trains, too, are many and varied, but in each case they should consist of wagons or cars that serve the needs of the layout. Thus, food, in meat and fish vans or in vegetable and milk wagons, together with general goods in parcels or utility vans, can be carried to all inhabited areas. Again, coal is an essential freight commodity and is taken in open wagons or in hopper cars to serve towns or loco sheds, power stations or lineside industries. All other cars serve special purposes; for example, salt wagons at salt works, ore cars at mines, fish vans at ports, and wine containers at vineyards.

Model classification

In the captions that follow, the Whyte classification of wheel arrangements is used, since it is more commonly used, both in the USA and in Britain for the description of steam locomotives. With this system of classification, the first figure indicates the number of pilot wheels, the second figure the driving wheels and the third figure the trailing wheels. On the Continent of Europe the number of axles is counted, so that a 4–6–2 would be a 2–C–1, the driving wheels being represented by the appropriate letter of the alphabet. The suffix T indicates a tank loco.

Diesel-Electric, Diesel-Mechanical, Electric and Gas-Turbine locos are classified differently, and here a number is allotted to each non-powered wheel and a letter for each powered wheel, as they are seen from one side. The suffix letter 'o' is added after the main letter to indicate a double-powered bogie (or truck), and if two bogies (powered or double-powered) are coupled by a drive shaft, a plus sign (+) is included in the classification. Let us take an example for explanation. Plate 49 shows a loco whose wheels would be described by Whyte as a 4–4–4–4, but in electric loco parlance as 2 – Bo + Bo – 2, indicating two non-powered two wheel bogies fore and aft, and two double-powered bogies in the centre, connected by a drive shaft.

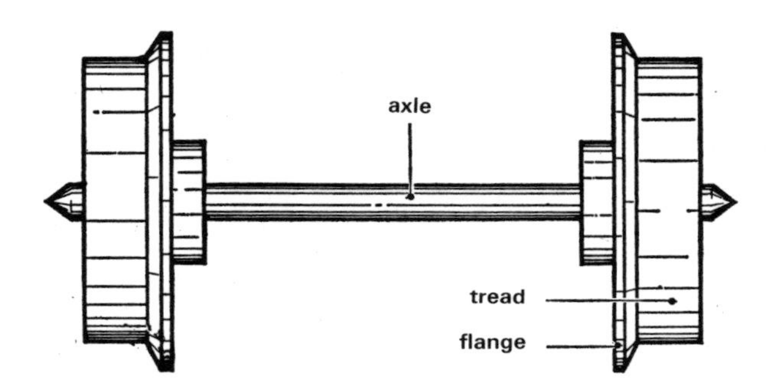

The most important dimensions of a model wheel are the overall width of the tire, the width, depth and shape of the flange, the width of the tread, the angle of the tread to the rail, and the back-to-back measurement of the two wheels on their axle.

Locomotives that bear certain types of wheel arrangements have been given specific names, eg:

2–4–2	Columbia	2–4–4	Hungary
2–6–0	Mogul	2–6–2	Prairie
2–6–4	Adriatic	2–6–6–6	Allegheny
2–8–0	Consolidation	2–8–2	Mikado
2–8–4	Berkshire	2–10–2	Santa Fe
2–10–4	Texas	2–12–4	Bulgaria
4–4–0	American	4–4–2	Atlantic
4–4–4	Dominion	4–6–2	Pacific
4–6–4	Hudson	4–6–6–4	Challenger
4–8–2	Mountain	4–8–4	Northern
4–8–8–4	Big Boy	4–10–0	Mastodon
4–10–2	Overland	4–14–4	Andriev

Finally, the types and styles of passenger cars and the liveries in use are faithfully reproduced in the shape and colourings used in the models illustrated. In Britain drab blue and grey have replaced the four distinct colourings common before 1948, but even these last could not compete with the tones, tints, shades and linings used by over 120 different railway companies before 1923, when they were grouped into the four major companies that lasted for the next quarter of a century.

Model railways is one of the world's most popular hobbies, claimed by some to be the biggest of all. Perhaps this book can help to show the newcomer some of the fascination which absorbs so many people in so many different countries.

Bibliography

Ahern, J. H., *Miniature landscape modelling*, Model & Allied Publishers (England)

Andress, M., *Narrow gauge model railways*, Almark (England)

Beal, E., *Railway modelling in miniature*, Model & Allied Publishers (England)

Carter, E. F., *The model railway encyclopedia*, Harold Starke (England)

Freezer, C. J., *A home for your railway*, Peco Publications (England)

Freezer, C. J., *Railway modeller shows you how booklets (20)*, Peco Publications (England)

Hertz, L. H., *The complete book of model railroading*, Simmons-Boardman (USA)

McClanahan, W., *Scenery for model railroads*, Kalmbach (USA)

Roche, F. J., and Templer, G. G., *Building model locomotives*, Ian Allen (England)

Simmons, N., *How to go railway modelling*, Patrick Stephens (England)

Sutton, D., *The complete book of model railroading*, Prentice Hall (USA)

Warren, R., *764 helpful hints for model railroaders*, Kalmbach (USA)

Westcott, L. H., *How to wire your model railroad*, Kalmbach (USA)

–2 The early railways are not quite as well represented in model form as erhaps they should be, but this is one example. The Trix Express replica of Der Adler' is slightly larger than the normal Continental scale of 3.5 mm to the oot because it would have been too small otherwise. The locomotive is not echanized, but is run by an electric motor in the second coach (the pick-up an be seen in front of the wheel).

The original 'Adler' opened the first German rail link between Fürth and Juremberg in 1835, and a hundred years later it was rebuilt. In 1960 it was ut back into service before being consigned to the Nuremberg transport useum.

This model shows the early type of passenger car, which consisted of one or ore mail-coach bodies of the sort drawn by horses.

1

2

3
4

3–4 The 'General' not only featured in a famous Buster Keaton film, but was part of an actual event during the American Civil War, during which it changed hands several times.

The Mantua Tyco model of this 4–4–0 American type locomotive features a 12 volt motor in the tender which drives the four main wheels via a rubber-shaft, visible in the photograph. The other locomotive which took part in the Keaton chase, the 'Texas', is also the subject of an HO Gauge model, as are a number of other American locomotives of the same era.

5

6

5 The superstructure of model locomotives is generally made of tin, a lead-tin alloy (often called 'white metal'), plastic compounds, or of copper sheet or brass as shown here. Different techniques of painting have to be used on these various surfaces. Many Japanese-built models of American locomotives, like the Tenshodo 0–4–0T Switcher shown here, are available in unpainted form.

6 A tank locomotive is one in which the supply of water is carried not in a separate tender but in tanks, which are described as pannier, saddle, or side. Shown is one of the four American tank locos, a Tenshodo 0–6–0T of a Baldwin Locomotive Works prototype.

7 Reclassified by the German Federal System as Class 89, several Class T3 0–6–0T tank locos of the old Prussian State Railways were still in service in 1963. The Fleischmann HO model has two operating headlights.

7

8 One of the older types of side-tank engines still in use with the Italian State Railways is the 0–6–0T Gr.835 loco used for shunting. This Rivarossi model is alongside one of the many different types of water-crane, this one modelled by Pocher.

9 The 0–6–0T Class 89 tank engine of the German Federal Railways appeared in 1927, and various versions with different sizes of side tanks were produced. An early version is shown in this Märklin model.

10 In 1922 the Italian State Railways Gr.940 type of tank loco was introduced for light passenger and freight service, and some are still serving in mountain regions of Italy. Only a few tank engines had the 2–8–2T ('Mikado') arrangement seen in this Rivarossi model.

11 The Tenshodo model of a 2–6–4T tank loco used mainly on iron ore trains of the Statens Järnvägar (Swedish State Railways) has a smart black livery and shows a certain amount of British influence.

12 13

12 Over 150 engines of the British Railways 4–MT (Power Classification 4–Mixed Traffic) 2–6–4T locomotives were built from 1948 onwards. They were developed from the London, Midland and Scottish Railway Stanier engines which were themselves originally taken from a large suburban passenger tank introduced by Sir Henry Fowler in 1927. The Hornby-Dublo model depicts this successful and extensive class of heavy tank.

13 A head-on-view of the Japanese-built model of the Swedish tank loco shown in Plate 11. Some fine detail can be observed, including the 'jewels' used as headlights.

14–15–16 The Altini model shown in these three pictures is of a steam engine with an unconventional form of motive power – a multi-cylinder steam locomotive with direct drive. The large inclined cylinders and the positions of the cranks can be clearly seen. The most modern locomotive of this kind was the (British) Southern Railway 'Leader' Class of 1948.

16

17 One of the most popular American models on model railroads is the diminutive switching engine. This example is the Rivarossi version of the Class C–16a of the Baltimore and Ohio railroad.

18 The 0–6–0 tender locomotives on American railroads were used for switching or for hauling light freight trains. This Altini model has a funnel used on wood-burning locos.

19

19 One of the smaller American railroads with only eighty route miles was the Maryland & Pennsylvania. This is a brass United model by Tenshodo of a 2–8–0 Consolidation used on short-run branch-line freight services in 1912.

20 In 1900 the famous Schenectady Locomotive Works built their 4–4–2 Atlantic, of which this is a collector's model, for the large Chicago and North Western Railway.

21 The 4–6–2 Pacific locomotive was one of the largest classes of locomotive built in the world, primarily for fast passenger trains. The American example modelled here was developed from the large-wheeled Atlantic depicted above.

20

21

22 The 2–8–2 Mikado, of which this is a Tenshodo model, was built in various versions including this heavy Class 0–8 (367,000 lbs), of which twenty-five operated on the Great Northern from 1932.

23 In 1929 the Baldwin Locomotive Works built six Class S–1 4–8–4 Northern locos for the Great Northern Railway Company which also featured a twelve-wheel Vanderbilt tender like that shown in Plate 22. This, too, is a Tenshodo model of a fast freight and passenger loco.

24–25–26 Two hundred and sixty 4–6–4 Hudson locomotives were built for the New York Central System. The Class J-3 was the final phase of this fine type, which replaced the 4–6–2 Pacific locos from 1927 onwards and which were themselves replaced by the 4–8–4 Northerns. (In Europe the 4–6–4 wheel arrangement is referred to as 'Baltic'.) The three views are of a Tenshodo model of a 1937 prototype.

NEW YORK CENTRAL
5428

27
28

27–28 The largest driving wheels used on a prototype engine of this type were the 74-inch diameter shown on the Tenshodo model of a 2–10–4 Texas type built in 1944 by Baldwin for the Atchison, Topeka & Santa Fe Railroad. This freight engine was derived from the earlier 2–10–2 Santa Fe type.

29 The Japanese firm of Tenshodo have made models of more than a hundred American locomotives; this is the front view of one of the large ones.

30 Among the larger compound Mallet articulated locos there are those with the following wheel arrangements: 2–8–8–0, 2–8–8–2, 2–8–8–4, 4–8–8–2 and 4–8–8–4 Big Boy. The Tenshodo model is of a 2–8–8–4 Class EM-1 of which the Baltimore and Ohio Railroad had thirty in service on coal trains in West Virginia in 1944. In a Mallet locomotive, both engines are placed under the boiler and the front one is on a separate bogie truck pivoted under the fore-part.

31

32

31 The Castle Class was one of the more successful locomotives built for a ailway, in this case the Great Western, which first appeared in 1924. This is a Hornby-Dublo model in early British Railways livery.

32 The A–4 Pacific was designed for high-speed passenger service between London and Newcastle for the London and North Eastern Railway. 'Mallard' of this class achieved 126 mph in 1938. Hornby-Dublo issued this garter-blue liveried version of the locomotive named after the A–4 designer.

33 Fleischmann have produced this model of a Class 41 2–8–2 of the German Federal Railways, complete with three headlights and smoke-deflectors. The prototype was used on long hauls for freight and occasionally for passenger trains in hilly regions.

34 The Prussian State Railways used a 4–6–0 Class 38 for mixed passenger and freight services. This Liliput model has a Seuthe smoke unit concealed in the boiler.

35

35 This is a Rivarossi model of a 2–8–0 freight locomotive, known as a type Gr.740, of the Italian State Railways. It is in the typical livery of black superstructure and red running plate, solebar and wheels.

36 The Gr.691 of the Italian State Railways was one of the more powerful of their steam locomotives. This is a Rivarossi model of the 4–6–2 Pacific which, until 1956, was still to be seen on main lines throughout Italy.

36

37

7 The Illinois Terminal Railroad is a freight line, most of which has been lectrified for some time. An overhead 600 volt system is used, and a model nade by Suydam of one of the early C Class B + B + B + B locos is shown here, omplete with two trolley poles.

8 Featuring a single pantograph with twin collectors, this is a Lionel model f a Co-Co locomotive of 3,300 hp for 11,000 volts single-phase, 25-cycle AC sed by the Virginian Railway Company, but here shown in the livery of the New York, New Haven & Hartford Railroad.

38

39 Märklin make this model of an electric shunting loco. It is a C Class E63 of the German Federal Railways with a gear-driven jackshaft.

40 The Bo+Bo German Federal Railways Class E44 was a general purpose electric locomotive for either suburban passenger or mixed freight trains. This model was made by Märklin.

41 A number of model manufacturers duplicate products. In this plate are the Trix Express (German) and Liliput (Austrian) versions of the Co+Co E94 electric goods locomotive which was the heaviest of its kind in 1940 when it went into service with the German Federal Railways, weighing 122 tons.

42 The Bo+Bo Class E40 of the German Federal Railways is in green (freight) livery. The prototype of the Fleischmann model weighs 185,136 lbs. The Class E10 passenger express loco is almost identical, and appears in several other liveries including blue, blue and ivory, and red and ivory.

43 The Class Ce 6/8 of the Swiss Federal Railway is an articulated 1–Co+Co–1 electric loco, nick-named the 'Crocodile' because of its appearance as it slides around the curves of the St Gotthard line. Märklin make this example of a heavy freight locomotive.

44

45

46

44 Forty-three multipurpose Class BB 12000 locos of the Bo-Bo wheel arrangement were built for the Paris–Lille line of the French National Railways. It weighs 76½ tons and in the blue livery shown hauls mineral wagons in eastern France on the Valenciennes–Thionville route. Fleischmann made this model.

45–46 Two views of the Pocher model of the Co-Co CC7101 locomotive are shown here. This type hauls express passenger trains on the Paris–Lyons line of the French National Railways at an average speed of 77 mph. Built by Alsthom, these locos have reached speeds of over 200 mph on several occasions since 1955.

47 Originally appearing in 1928 for use in southern Italy on heavy freight trains, the Gr.E626 of the Italian State Railways is in two halves, being articulated. This Bo + Bo + Bo loco, of which a Rivarossi model is shown, was followed by the similar E636 built in both freight and passenger versions, with differing transmission ratios.

48 The Class E424 Bo + Bo modelled here by Märklin appeared in 1943 and is commonly used all over Italy on light freight or light passenger duties.

47

48

49

50

51

49–50 There have been three series of the Italian State Railways Class E428 2–Bo + Bo–2 loco. Rivarossi make models of all three. Both the model in Plate 49 and the Fleischmann version in Plate 50 are of the Series II, with an articulated underframe. The prototype has eight electric motors. The three series may be identified by the progressive improvement in the streamlining.

51 In 1959 the Class E646 Bo + Bo + Bo appeared on the Italian State Railways. Rivarossi built this model featuring the articulated arrangement visible here. It was used on the heavier passenger and freight trains.

52 Rivarossi also model the second series of the Class E646 of the Italian State Railways which has a different shape of cab (at each end) from the earlier engines. It is probably the most powerful of present-day Italian electric locomotives.

52

53 54

53 The Baldwin-Westinghouse Model S-12 1200 hp switching locomotive was bought by over seventy railroads in the USA. Fleischmann used to make the B-B model shown here in two of the many liveries employed.

54 Tenshodo models of the Electro-Motive Division of General Motors Corporation's GP–9 (general purpose) and SD–9 (special duty hood unit). These B–B and C–C locos are road switchers for operating in yards. They spelt the end of the American steam loco by reason of their superior operational ability.

55 Tenshodo and Rivarossi models of the EMD–General Motors B–B Model F–7 of 1500 hp are shown below. Designed for heavy duty passenger service as well as for their primary function as pullers of freight, these locos are available in A (with a cab) or B units. These may be coupled A–A, A–B, A–B–B, A–B–B–A, or A–B–A, to give up to 6,000 hp. Over sixty US railroads use these locomotives.

56 The Krupp works in Essen builds the Class V60 diesel switcher, which is classified C and has a blind-shaft drive. Of 650 hp, this German Federal Railways loco is used in yards. The model is by Fleischmann.

57 Of the classic shape to be seen on several European railways, Märklin's model of the German Federal Railways Class V200 Bo + Bo diesel is similar in outline to the British Rail type 4 B–B 'Warship' Class of 2,200 brake horse-power.

58

59

60

58 In 1953 British Railways introduced an 0–6–0 diesel shunter. Over a thousand were built of Classes 08, 09 and in 1955, ten of this ubiquitous 350 bhp locomotive, of which Hornby-Dublo made the model here.

59 Over twenty Class 55 'Deltic' locos have been put into service by British Railways (later British Rail) since 1961, each powered by two Napier Deltic engines of 1,650 bhp. The Co-Co here is by Hornby-Dublo.

60 Used on secondary lines for passenger and freight services is the Class D342 of the Italian State Railways. This diesel locomotive model is made by Lima.

61 Diesel railcars of the German type shown here are normally used in single or twin units (one motor car and one trailer) on local suburban services. This is a Fleischmann model.

62 The Fiat 7145B made for the Italian State Railways is available in two colour schemes from Rivarossi. The prototype motor coach ALn 668 may have a trailer.

63 Electric railcars also exist in some countries and the Altini model of a twin-articulated unit using three trucks is similar to other European motor coaches.

61

62

63

64

65

66

64 Many old passenger coaches had a clerestory (clear story) – a row of long windows raised above the roof line – for ventilation, as is seen in this Pocher model of a Swedish State Railways Type C third class coach.

65 Fleischmann modelled this second and third class coach, Class BCi Pr 98a of the former Prussian State Railways. This was an 1878 coach.

66 In the background is a Fleischmann model of a baggage and mail car, class Pw Posti Pr 92 of the Prussian State Railways, and in front of it is a Märklin model of a six-wheeled (later Class C3) Prussian compartment coach. The prototype was dull grey and there were four classes of travel, of which the fourth was very primitive.

67

68

67 The green coach on the left is a Fleischmann model of a Class Bymb second class coach of the German Federal Railway. On the right is a Rivarossi model of a Class Bz second class coach of the Italian State Railways.

68 Comparison between two different scales is shown in this photograph of a Fleischmann HO Gauge model which is 9⅜ inches in length overall, and a 5½ inch long N Gauge model by Arnold-Rapido, both of a Trans-Europ Express car, Class AV4um. (Both cars are first class, the former with compartments and the latter with a centre aisle.)

69 The chocolate and cream livery of the early Western Region, contrasting with the plum colour of the Midland Region coaches in the 1950s shows in this photograph of Hornby-Dublo tinplate models of British Railways passenger rolling stock.

70 In front is a HOrnby-acHO model of a second class French National Railways coach. This is an older type of vehicle.

71

72

71 This is a Rivarossi model of a first class coach of the Italian State Railways, type Az 52000. The Bz 31000 second class car is similar, but has a centre aisle and not compartments.

72 Pocher also makes models of the Az 52000 first class and Bz 31000 second class coaches of the Italian State Railways in the dark and bright blue livery used experimentally in the fifties, as well as in brown and fawn (see Plate 71).

NEW HAVEN
N H
PULLMAN
ST. CROIX
BAGGAGE
AMERICAN RAILWAY
EXPRESS
SANTA FE
UNITED STATES MAIL
RAILWAY POST OFFICE
SANTA FE
30293

3 Fleischmann made these models of a passenger coach and a baggage-oach combine in the livery of the New York, New Haven & Hartford ailroad.

4 These are Athearn models of 'standard coaches', a dining car and a aggage-mail combine of the Atchison, Topeka & Santa Fe Railroad.

5 Streamlined cars followed the 'standard coaches', and Tenshodo modelled streamlined observation car shown here with an observation dome. This also ppeared on the Santa Fe Railroad.

76 The International Sleeping Car Company has blue and white Pullman cars, blue restaurant cars, and blue baggage cars. These are Pocher models.

77 Liliput make models of earlier cars used by the international companies on European expresses. The blue one is a Pullman, and the teak coloured coach is a dining car of the Swiss Federal Railways on the St Gotthard Line.

COMPAGNIE INTERNATIONALE DES WAGONS-LITS ET DES GRANDS EXPRESS EUROPEENS
SLEEPING-CAR
SCHLAFWAGEN

78

SCHLAFWAGEN
D S G
SCHLAFWAGEN

79

80

SBB CFF

78 The International Sleeping Car Company has introduced modern equipment in recent years. The model by Pocher is of a sleeping-car made by Fiat, type 15G no 4581.

79 The German Sleeping Car and Dining Car Company (DSG) uses sleeping cars like this Pocher model of a class WLAB4um. Both first class and second class versions exist.

80 In front is a Märklin model of a German Federal Railways goods traffic luggage van, type Pwg. Behind is a Pocher model of a Swiss Federal Railways Class Fz4ü baggage and post van.

81 This is the famous Armistice Coach. An old dining car of the International Sleeping Car Company, No. 2419 was used both in 1918 and in 1940 for the signing of Armistices between France and Germany. It no longer exists. The Germans blew up the museum in which it was housed near Compiègne in 1940, and destroyed the car itself in 1945 at Ohrdruf. The Pocher model shown here is complete with all the interior fittings of the original teak vehicle.

82 An unusual model, by Pocher, is of the car used by President Lincoln on his train trips in the USA. It has four bogies or trucks for smooth riding and to support the weight of the fittings.

89 In the foreground are two type Poz 1920 flat cars (seen in the previous plate) used together with military models by Lesney and Micromodels. The 2–8–2T tank loco is a model by Rivarossi of the Italian State Railways Class 940. The coach is by Lima.

90 The Red Cross or hospital train is made up of some of the early Lima models of cars and vans.

91 These models of Italian wagons are by various manufacturers. The attractive crane wagon is by Pocher. Other models are by Electrotren, Lima and Rivarossi.

92 Tram locomotives have appeared in various countries. This Lima model is typical of the narrow gauge trains used on local lines in Europe, hauling two or three small passenger cars. The track gauge of this model is 9 mm.

93 This is a tram, trolley-car or interurban, made by Tenshodo. With their standard gauge of 4 feet 8½ inches, trams were used a great deal in metropolitan cities until ousted by the diesel-engined omnibus. Pickup was from overhead wire or via a carrier running in a slot in a centre rail.

93

94 In Germany many trams hauled single-deck trailers. This is a Hamo model.

95 In Milan earlier this century, tramcars of the Edison type were used, sometimes pulling a trailer car. This is a Rivarossi model, for which special road sections with inset rail are available.

96

96 Among the many models of figures available in various scales are those of Merit and Prieser (shown here), and Merten, Airfix and Peco.

97 Each of these points, turnouts or switches is for remote control, and contains solenoids which operate spring-loaded closure rails. The Märklin points with stud contacts are shown on the left, the first being scale model track and the other standard track. Next is a Fleischmann point which has four spring clips. Wires attached to different clips and various accessories enable various forms of automatic operation. On the right is a Trix Express point with a centre third rail, actually the common return, as each of the outer rails is used for independent pickups.

97

98

99

100

101

98 Fleischmann makes this particular model of he 90-ton German Type 6700 Nür crane. The omplete model consists of the crane-car tender to upport the boom in transit, the idler car carrying vood blocks (at the back on the right), the crane ar itself, and the counterweight car; the weights re missing in this photograph.

99 Just about every type of bridge is available or model railway enthusiasts. This is a single span irder bridge, but there are short-arch girders with ows above or below, long box-girder bridges, iaducts, timber trestle bridges, and so on.

100 Tunnel mouths, like this Faller model, of arious kinds, compositions and shapes are also btainable. (The VT 45 railcar in the livery of the ustrian Federal Railways, is a Lima model.)

101 Scenery adds to the realism of a model. The uildings are by Kibri, the trees by Britains and aller, the figures by Merit, and the rocks are atural.

102

103

104

02–103 Two more views of the scene shown in 'late 101 give an overall impression of an Alpine ailway station.

04 This freight station has Märklin track, ollmer buildings, HOrnby acHO signals, a ivarossi loco, and wagons by various makers.

05 The Märklin goods van is being loaded with lerit freight.

06 An unusual scene is this Pocher closed oods wagon being conveyed on a road trailer.

105

106

107

108

109

110

07 This is a model of a Continental railway station, a continuation of which can be seen in the next photograph.

08 Models by various manufacturers have been used to compose this station scene, of which a third view is in the next plate.

109 The number of model trains in the station gives an air of activity to the picture.

110 On the right foreground is a transformer. There are controllers on both sides of the panel. The Märklin switch panels in blue cases are for switching on or off the train and lighting circuits; the two with green buttons on the right operate points and signals. The eleven distributor panels for the sections are in the centre.

111–112 By day or by night, with or without model people, a model railway station holds the attention of the spectator.

111–112

Two Southern Railways Schools Class 4-4-0s at Waterloo both on Portsmouth trains.

Schools Class 4-4-0 No.30928 'Stowe' is seen passing Paddock Wood with a Dover–Victoria express. The coal wagon and sidings for mixed freight eloquently remind us how the Railway provided an efficient co-ordinated transport system in those glorious pre-motorway days.

31745

An unidentified Drummond T9 Class 4-4-0 drifts down the 1 in 37 bank from Exeter Central to Exeter St David's on a Plymouth train.

Bulleid Battle of Britain Class 4-6-2 No.34084 "253 Squadron" heads a Victoria-Dover express past Minster Junction having taken the S.E.R. route via Ashford.

Opposite
Re-built Class D1, 4-4-0 No.31743 pauses at Canterbury East on a stopping train to Ramsgate via the S.E.R. route.

GUILDFORD
33004

GUILDFORD
WY 43

A Southern Railway rail built upper quadrant signal frames H Class 0-4-4T No.31519 propelling a pull and push train to Oxted.

Previous spread
Two Schools Class 4-4-0s run neck and neck between Hither Green and Grove Park. On the slow line No.900 "Eton" is working a Charing Cross-Dover train, while No.906 "Sherborne" heads a Cannon Street-Hastings Train on the fast line.

Over page
One of Bulleid's powerful wartime Austerity 0-6-0s of Class Q1, No.33004, shunts a covered wagon at the south end of Guildford Station.

A pleasant scene on the S.E.R. main line in Kent with Ashford based King Arthur Class 4-6-0 No.30803 “Sir Harry le Fiselake”.

Hard working re-built West Country Class 4-6-2 No.34034 “Honiton” passes Mitcheldever at speed with a down Ocean Liner Express to Southampton docks, the Pullman cars suggesting it was a Cunard working.

LMS
L M S
ALBERT USHER
LONDON
906

71
Nº 900

An interesting comparison of two railway's main line goods engines at Stewarts Lane shed Battersea. At left ex-S.E.C.R. Wainwright Class C, 0-6-0 No.31724 at right ex-L.B.S.C.R. Class C2x, 0-6-0 No. 32437. There was not a lot to choose between them but each railway's drivers preferred their own. In World War One, both companies introduced 2-6-0s for heavy freight work. Above, a King Arthur Class 4-6-0 heads a down express.

A party visit to Hither Green Shed with cameras focused on an N Class 2-6-0 as a C Class 0-6-0 simmers alongside.

Shed shunting in progress at Ramsgate Shed, with the engines in wartime black livery. At left re-boilered Stirling Class B1, 4-4-0 No.1452 (withdrawn in 1950), while a Class C, 0-6-0 shunts Class H, 0-4-4T No.1523. In the distance on the turntable stands a Class L1 4-4-0.

The N Class Moguls were predominant in workings over the Reading-Redhill line. Here No.31411, one of the last batch to be built in 1933, heads a train through Gomshall and Shere.

Opposite
A Bulleid Battle of Britain Class Pacific nears the end of it's journey as it enters Birchington on Sea with a Victoria-Ramsgate express.

Previous spread
A D1 Class 4-4-0 with a lattice post London Chatham and Dover Railway signal.

Over page
A scene in the shed yard at Ramsgate with a Schools Class 4-4-0 taking coal. At right a Class H 0-4-4T and a Class T9 4-4-0 complete this pre-war view.

WAITING ROOM
GENTLEMEN
WAY OUT & LADIES ROOM
OUT

31505
264

Schools Class No.30920 "Rugby" couples on to a boat train at Folkestone Junction.

South Eastern and Chatham Class D1, 4-4-0 No.31749 heads an up train at Sittingbourne Junction (for Sheerness).

Class M7, 0-4-4T No.30047 heads a pull and push train to Brighton at Horsham Station, which was re-built in 1938 for the Mid-Sussex line electrification.

A South Eastern and Chatham H Class 0-4-4T at Minster.

Canterbury West signal box with Classes H 0-4-4T and N 2-6-0 visible. The old Canterbury and Whitstable Railway engine shed can be seen in the background.

The Erecting Shop at Eastleigh Works. Left and centre are two Class H15 4-6-0s, at right King Arthur Class 4-6-0 No.788 "Sir Urre of the Mount" still in wartime black livery.

Ashford Works Erecting Shop with Wainwright Class C, 0-6-0 No.1691.

Stirling Class QI 0-4-4T No.A423 after its 1926 withdrawal was modified at Ashford Works for a stationary steam provision in which form it survived until 1933. This is surely one of Arthur Mace's most exciting pictures.

Previous spread

At Cannon Street, newly built Battle of Britain Class 4-6-2 No.21C167 "Tangmere" heads a down Dover express in the evening rush hour. This engine in un-rebuilt condition is undergoing restoration on the Mid Hants Railway.

SOUTHERN
469
s 21C167

Two re-boilered Stirling Class R1, 0-6-0Ts, Nos.1337 and 1174, head an up continental express from Folkestone Harbour. A third 0-6-0T would be banking in the rear. At Folkestone Junction, a main line engine would take over. These elderly engines were replaced by surplus W.R. 0-6-0PT s in 1959 until electrification in 1961.

SOUTHERN
1337
SOUTHERN
1174

Between April and June 1948, two L.M.R. 2-6-4Ts, No's.42198/99, were loaned to the S.R. for trials, largely between Waterloo and Basingstoke and Victoria and Tunbridge Wells West. However, on 23rd and 24th April, No.42199 was tested between Victoria and Ashford via Maidstone East. It is seen leaving Ashford for London.

Dramatic picture of an Ashford based Wainwright Class D, 4-4-0 on a Ramsgate-Victoria train. In pre-war days, a Pullman car was included on certain services on this route.

A busy scene at the Margate end of Ramsgate Station. Perhaps the coaling plant was out of order as engines are being coaled by crane on the right hand side. In the platform stands a Class D1 4-4-0 and at left a Class H 0-4-4T.

Brighton-Cardiff through train near Lancing in the charge of West Country Class 4-6-2 No.34048 "Crediton" with G.W.R. carriages. The S.R. engine worked through to Salisbury.

The same location, West Country Class 4-6-2 No.34039 "Boscastle" heads the Brighton-Plymouth through train. Sets of pictures from the same location were a characteristic of Arthur Mace's work.

Bulleid West Country Class Pacific No.34100 "Appledore" heads for London via Folkestone near Hawkesbury Street Junction. This once facinating area is now largely superseded by the Channel Tunnel. At right, behind the footbridge, the tracks lead into Dover Western Docks station recently closed.

Two Adams express locomotives of the mid 1890's await scrap at Eastleigh after the war. These 6' 6" 4-4-0s were T3 Class No.571 and X6 Class No.666. The former class is represented by No.563 in the National Railway Museum in York.

The Golden Years of British Steam Trains

SR

SOUTHERN RAILWAY

MILEPOST

In snow and so probably close to Arthur Mace's home at Rugby, Class O4/3, 2-8-0 No.3681 of Gorton heads a Great Central Line freight. These original Great Central engines were built between 1911/20 many for the Railway Operating Division during World War One. Under this guise the type saw widespread service overseas. Most were purchased back into L.N.E.R. stock in the 1920s. The type saw considerable re-building culminating in an almost complete transformation by Thompson, but many survived largely as built including the example shown here.

THE
MASTER CUTLER
61376

Class J25 0-6-0 No.5665 heads a mineral train through Barnard Castle. Forty of these engines were loaned to the G.W.R. in World War Two to compensate for the loss of Dean Goods 0-6-0s to the War Department. As L.N.E.R. No.1991 prior to the 1946 renumbering, this engine stayed on its home patch.

Ex-North British Railway Class D30, 4-4-0 No.62423 "Dugald Dalgetty" of Hawick heads a short freight. The engine appears to have a badly scorched smokebox door.

Although almost exclusively on the L.N.E.R. system, a few War Department Austerity 2-8-0s were allocated to the Great Western. Here, Shrewsbury based No. 90261 enters Leamington Spa on a down freight train. Notice the G.W.R. type top feed fitted to those engines working on W.R. lines.

Thompson O1 Class 2-8-0 No.63755 was one of five engines fitted with continuous vacuum brake and Westinghouse pumps to work iron ore trains from Tyne dock to Consett. The O1s were Thompson re-builds of Robinson's original Great Central 2-8-0s. This heavy drag of iron ore is being banked by an ex-North Eastern Railway Q7 0-8-0.

Over page

The rural character of the former Great Central Main Line is evidenced here as Thompson Class B1 4-6-0 No.61371 of Leicester 38C was recorded working hard on the Sheffield to Marylebone "Master Cutler" Express.

The gracefulness of the Great Central Atlantics is evident despite the advancing years as Class C4, 4-4-2 No.5360 heads an express south of Rugby along the Great Central Main Line. Built at Gorton in 1906, this engine survived until 1948. The ridge and furrow field alongside has survived since medieval times and is referred to in Sir John Betjeman's poem "The Great Central Railway".

The ridge and furrow formations are evident again in this war time scene at the same location featuring neglected Great Central section Pacific No.4471 "Sir Frederick Banbury" seen rather uncharacteristically at the head of a goods train.

A Class B12/3, 4-6-0 heads a through train on the M.& G.N. joint line near Sheringham.

Previous spread
Built in 1923, No.60108 "Gay Crusader" (1917 Derby winner) stands at the buffer stops of Kings Cross. Formally L.N.E.R. Class A3 No.4477, it was withdrawn in 1963 having been replaced by Deltics on the East Coast Main Line.

60108
LONDON

Great Northern stalwarts at Nottingham Victoria. On the far left is a K2 Class "Ragtimer" along with a pair of Ivatt J6 Class 0-6-0s.

Another K2 Class "Ragtimer" in the form of No.61773 based at Colwick Depot Nottingham, at the head of a Nottingham to Grantham train.

Gorton based ex-G.C.R. Class C13, 4-4-2T No.6058, withdrawn in 1955 as B.R. No. 67403, heads a local passenger train out of Manchester London Road. A Class B3 4-6-0 waits with a later departure.

A rare wartime view of the same location - almost certainly near Rugby - with ex-Great Central Railway 4-6-0 No.5195 of Class B1 (later reclassified B18) piloting Class V2, 2-6-2 No.4820 with an ambulance train proceeded by three Southern Railway carriages. Wartime photography was severely restricted so one hopes that none of the occupants of the houses reported Arthur Mace's activities.

Years later in B.R. days, Class B1, 4-6-0 No.61131 heads a special train of L.M.R. stock. The location has altered little, but the all pervading B1's quickly decimated most of the older classes on the former Great Central section.

Over page
A grimy looking Peppercorn Class K1, 2-6-0 on freight duty in the North East.

The second of Gresley's Great Northern Railway built Pacifics was No.60102 "Sir Frederick Banbury". During its later years, it was transferred to the Great Central section and allocated to Leicester. It is seen here working the South Yorkshireman.

Class A3, 4-6-2 No.2750 "Papyrus" also at Kings Cross Shed was built in 1929 and bears the Scarborough Flyer headboard. This engine achieved fame in 1935 when it made high speed runs between Kings Cross and Newcastle in 3 hours 47½ minutes, so paving the way for the L.N.E.R.'s first streamlined express The Silver Jubilee later that year.

Another celebrated L.N.E.R. Pacific was A4 "Silver Link". During trial running of the Silver Jubilee in September 1935 this engine twice attained 112½ miles an hour and over a 10.6 mile stretch averaged 108.7 miles an hour.

The G.N.R. Klondyke 4-4-2s - so named because of their emergence in 1897 followed the great Gold Rush to the Yukon - were the first Atlantics in Britain. Only twenty two were built and they were soon eclipsed by the large boilered Atlantics, the first of which appeared five years later. Hitchin based Class C2, 4-4-2 No.3982 is seen on the turntable at Kings Cross Shed. The engine survived until 1935.

Large boiler Ivatt Class C1, 4-4-2 No.4434 was built in 1907 and was no doubt recorded by Arthur Mace at Kings Cross on the same occasion. Succeeded by the Pacifics on the East Coast Main Line it was withdrawn in 1945.

Gresley designed the powerful K3 Class 2-6-0s of which nearly two hundred were built between 1920 and 1937. They were superb mixed traffic engines and a worthy precursor to Gresley's later V2 2-6-2s. No.114, later B.R. No.61831, was built in 1924 and remained active until 1962.

Another scene at Doncaster works, this one in the Erecting Shop where one of the later built K3, Class 2-6-0s No.61959 of 1936 vintage awaits a light repair. At the time this picture was taken, No. 61959 was allocated to Lowestoft.

Previous spread
A G.C.R. 2-8-0 of class 04 heads a fitted freight train of perishables. This class was built in large numbers for use overseas in World War I.

The end of the road - Gresley Class N2, 0-6-2T No's.69557 and 69566 on the scrap line at Doncaster works. Built in 1925, they were withdrawn in 1957.

The boiler shop at Doncaster works.

Ex-North British Railway 4-4-0 No.62485 "Glen Murran" of Class D34 pauses with a train at Edinburgh Waverley.

Hull based War Department Austerity 2-8-0 No.90688 passes through Beverley Road with a freight train.

Former North Eastern Railway 4-6-0 No.929 of Class B16 at York Station. Built in 1921, this handsome engine was withdrawn as No.61424 in 1960.

Ex-North British Railway 0-6-0 No.5267 was built at Cowlairs in 1892. She belonged to Class J36 which consisted of 168 engines.

427

Ex-North British Railway Class J88, 0-6-0T No.9235 of 1909, shunts at Leith docks. As B.R. No.68334 the engine survived until 1959. Introduced by Reid, these dock tanks with 3' 9" diameter wheels were built between 1915/1919. All had vanished by 1962.

Over page
Ivatt large boilered Atlantic Class C1, 4-4-2 No.4427 heads a stopping passenger train near Cambridge. These large boilered engines, introduced in 1902 revolutionised express passenger services on the Great Northern and much publicity was made about the girth of their boilers. When Nigel Gresley succeeded Henry Ivatt as Chief Mechanical Engineer of the Great Northern Railway, he modified the engines with high degree superheating which made their performance even more dynamic and on many occasions they deputised sucessfully for Pacifics on the heavy Anglo Scottish expresses. The first of these engines was withdrawn in 1943 and, literally worn out from years of hard work, the remainder followed, the last one disappearing in 1950.

Manning Wardle built 0-4-2T No.8192 of Class Z5, one of two built for use at Aberdeen docks. It was withdrawn in 1960.

Both these engines were based at Kittybrewster with two similar engines of Class Z4. No.8193, also seen at Aberdeen, was withdrawn in 1956.

Heading for Liverpool Street, Class N7 0-6-2T No.2615 leaves Stratford with a train of G.E.R. suburban stock.

Ex-N.B.R Class C15, 4-4-2T No.67460 pauses on the Caigendoran-Arrochar and Tarbet push and pull service.

Ex-G.N.R. J6 Class 0-6-0 No.64267 was one of the last survivors of its class and was allocated to Colwick Depot, Nottingham.

Ex-North British Railway Class D34, 4-4-0 No.2426 "Cuddie Headrigg" of Perth heads a local passenger train.

Arthur Mace has caught the essence of a country branch line with this scene at the terminus of the Easingwold Railway which ran for some two miles from Alne on the East Coast Main Line. In 1947, the railway's Hudswell Clark, 0-6-0T needed extensive repair and a class J71 or J72 was hired from York. Here, Class J71 0-6-0T No.68246 stands with the railway's ex-G.C.R. coach. The line closed in 1957.

935 of these Austerity 2-8-0s were built for the War Department during World War Two. After service abroad, most returned to B.R. and here No.90582 of Mexborough is seen hauling a freight on the Great Central Main Line. No British locomotives were as neglected as these Austerities. They were always filthy with cabside numbers indicipherable. They could be heard approaching over long distances by the heavy 'plonk' of banging bushes. An Austerity version of Stanier's L.M.S. 8F 2-8-0 they lacked any family lineage and were stark austere machines. They had few devotees and yet were one of the most exciting classes for trainspotters as 773 of them roamed Britain working from dozens of different sheds. Their tasks often involved inter colliery transfers and they had the delightful habit of turning up miles off their home territory.

Thompson Class L1 2-6-4T No.67758 of Neasden, hauls a train of ex-L.M.S. non corridor stock through the outer suburbs of London.

Gorton based Thompson B1 Class No.61265 at the head of an excursion composed of ex-L.M.S. corridor stock. Between 1942 and 1950, 410 of these general purpose engines were built.

Later in 1938, the Stirling Single ran a special to and from Cambridge with the old stock. This was organised by the R.C.T.S.

No.1 backs on to its train at Kings Cross with admiring glances from all occupants of the platform along with the crew of Class N2, 0-6-2T No.4766.

Opposite
Prior to the 1938 acceleration of the Flying Scotsman, a replica of the 1888 train of seven 6 wheeled coaches was hauled by the preserved Stirling Single 4-2-2 No.1 which was specially brought out of the old York museum and overhauled. It ran from Kings Cross as far as Stevenage, where guests transferred to the new train.

L N E R
4766
No 1

Cambridge engines started working one through train over the former London & North Western line to Oxford in 1954. Here, Class D16/3, 4-4-0 No.62585 leaves Oxford on the return journey.

Opposite
In un-rebuilt form with A.C.F.I. feed water heater, Class B12, 4-6-0 No.8569 heads a Kings Cross buffet car express. It was re-built as Class B12/3 in 1933 and, as No.61569 was withdrawn in 1957.

The up Flying Scotsman approaches York behind the record breaking Class A3 Pacific No.2750 "Papyrus".

An A1 Pacific speeds through Durham with an up express.

Over page
At Kings Cross shed Class J52, 0-6-0T No.4213 stands beside a large boilered Ivatt Atlantic. Unusually for a London based engine, the J52 is not fitted with condensing gear. As No.68800 it was withdrawn in 1958.

A post war view of Class A4 Pacific No.60009 "Union of South Africa" entering Newcastle on the Flying Scotsman.

Durham Station in L.N.E.R. days with a V2, 2-6-2 on the left and an A3 Pacific.

One of Arthur Mace's most exciting pictures and dated 1946/7. The Gresley V2, 2-6-2 has drawn well up in the platform and threatens to obscure the view of the A4 Pacific approaching at speed much to the chagrin of the train spotters who are in a clear state of emotional agitation.

WOODFOR

Ex-Great Central Railway Class N5 0-6-2T No.9352, and Class C13, 4-4-2T No.67417 stand on local trains in the Cheshire Lines Committee terminus at Chester Northgate.

The symmetry of a 4-4-4T was a joy to behold and here North Eastern Railway Class H1, No.2147 is in her original form at York prior to being re-built as a 4-6-2T. She survived in re-built form as No.69854 until 1960.

L.N.E.R. Class A8, 4-6-2T No.9851 at Newcastle. These engines originally comprised a class of 45 4-4-4Ts built for the North Eastern Railway between 1913 and 1922. All were re-built to 4-6-2T's during the 1930's.

Over page
A sad state for one of the graceful Great Central Railway Class C4, 4-4-2s known as Jersey Lilies. The engine is seen here receiving attention on the sheerlegs at Woodford shortly before her withdrawal in the late 1940's.

INTRODUCTION

The L.N.E.R was the second largest of the Big Four companies. It inherited a remarkable range of locomotives from such major pre-grouping companies as the Great Northern, Great Eastern, Great Central, North Eastern and North British. It's territory ranged from London and East Anglia to Aberdeen and beyond. Rivalry with the L.M.S. for services between London and Scotland was legendary and dated back to the exciting railway races of 1888 and 1895 which were performed by the coordinated efforts of major railway companies on either side of Britain.

The L.N.E.R.'s locomotive giant was Nigel Gresley, who took over as Chief Mechanical Engineer from the outset having previously held that position on the Great Northern Railway. Gresley's big designs are amongst the most famous in railway history, especially his A3 and A4 Pacifics whilst lesser known designs, like his mighty P1/P2 2-8-2s of 1925, were equally awe inspiring.

The L.N.E.R. did not pursue locomotive standardisation so vigorously as the other companies and it was not until Edward Thompson took over as chief Mechanical Engineer in 1941 that the B1 mixed traffic 4-6-0s were introduced and rapidly decimated a vast array of older types. In spite of this, nationalisation saw the L.N.E.R. hand over to British Railways an incredible 150 different classes totalling 6,550 locomotives.

Profile of a Class N2, 0-6-2T No.69498, having brought in empty stock to Kings Cross terminus.

Opposite
A pair of Thompson engines caught in begrimed condition towards the end of steam. On the left is Class L1, 2-6-4T No.67740 with a B1 Class 4-6-0.

Previous spread
A wartime view at the north end of York Station. Class A4, 4-6-2 No.4499, "Sir Murrough Wilson" on a northbound train while a grimy Class V2, 2-6-2 heads south.

The Golden Years of British Steam Trains

LNER

LONDON & NORTH EASTERN RAILWAY

LNWR George V Class 4-4-0 No. 25376 "Snipe", a Chester engine, stands on an express passenger train.

The introduction of Stanier's designs during the 1930's led to either the withdrawal of former LNW express passenger designs or their relegation to secondary work as in this instance of Bletchley based 4-6-0 No. 25673 "Lusitania" ekeing out her final days in the post war period with a stopping passenger train.

Previous spread

Ex-L&YR 2-4-2T No. 10872 allocated to Agecroft shed Salford, heads a local passenger train at Manchester Victoria while a near relative in the form of L&YR 0-6-0 No. 52300 stands on a parcels train.

12300

10872
10872
L M S

An ex-L&YR 4-4-2 "High Flyer" Atlantic shunting empty stock. Forty of these fast running engines were built between 1899 and 1902, the last one being withdrawn in 1934.

Arthur Mace's station scenes represent some of his most exciting work. Some are topographical, others feature people very prominently as in this one revealing a parade of light engines passing through Rugby led by Nuneaton based Hughes Crab 2-6-0 No. 42888.

THE LINE BY THE BRIDGE
3 4 5 & 6 & BAYS 3 4 5 6 9 & 10
LONDON BIRMINGHAM & THE SOUTH
BRISTOL AND THE WEST OF ENGLAND
CENTRAL WALES CAMBRIAN
& NORTH STAFFORDSHIRE LINES
REFRESHMENT ROOM

A former L&NWR 4-4-0 heads an express passenger train round the curve into Chester.

Previous spread
Another scene taken from one of Arthur Mace's post war 35mm negatives reveals ex-LNWR Prince of Wales Class 4-6-0 No. 25673 "Lusitania". This engine was one of the last two Prince of Wales to remain in service being withdrawn in 1949. The generic LNWR family likeness with the 0-8-0 in the background is unmistakable.

Over page
Hughes 4-6-0 No. 10452 built by the LMS to L&YR design stands in Crewe Station at the head of an express for Carlisle. After a remarkably short working life, this engine was withdrawn in 1936.

An exhibition of locomotives and rolling stock was held at Euston in 1938 to commemorate the centenary of the London and Birmingham Railway. This prestigious line-up is led by Liverpool and Manchester Railway 0-4-2 "Lion" of 1838; Princess Coronation Class 4-6-2 No. 6225 "Duchess of Gloucester" of 1938; George V Class 4-4-0 No. 25348 "Coronation" of 1911 and 2-2-2 "Cornwall" of 1847.

At the British Empire Exhibition at Wembley in 1924, ex-LNWR, 2-2-2 "Columbine" was dwarfed by LMS No. 11114, a 4-6-4T of L&YR design built in that year.

73

This London and North Western scene at Shrewsbury is another of Arthur Mace's North Wales classics. On the left is an ex-L.N.W.R. Webb 2-4-2T seen with one of that designer's slightly earlier 0-6-2T Coal Tanks.

One of Webb's ubiquitous London and North Western Coal Tank 0-6-2Ts which formed a class of 300 locomotives built between 1881 and 1896. Once prolific across the vast London and North Western territories, most of the last survivors ended their days in Wales working two or three coach branch line trains as depicted here at an unknown location. All survivors had gone by 1958.

The evacuation special of Dulwich College Prep School to Betsycoed from West Dulwich in 1942. The L.N.W.R. Coal Tank seen here would have taken over at Llandudno Jnc. 1995 was the 50th Anniversary of the boys return to Dulwich.

Previous spread
Shrewsbury based Ivatt Class 2, 2-6-2T No. 41203 is the subject of much interest from the local train spotters as it stands at the lengthy platform at Kidderminster with a Severn Valley Line train.

41203
BR (W)

Another Crewe Works shunter of the same period was LNWR Coal Engine, 0-6-0 No. 8245 built in 1889. Not officially regarded as service stock, the engine acquired its BR number 58347. This engine, along with several sisters, survived on internal duties at Crewe long after other members of the class had been withdrawn finally disappearing in 1953.

Crewe Works also employed LNWR special tank number 27334 "Liverpool". This 1867 built engine survived until 1939.

An ex-works repaint at Crewe for Class G2A 0-8-0 number 48899. Built as a Webb Compound in 1904, she was converted to simple expansion 3 years later and was finally re-built with Belpaire boiler in 1941.

Ex-North London Railway's 0-6-0T No. 27514. Although several were transferred to the Crompton and High Peak line based on Rowsley, this engine remained on its native territory at Devons Road Bow.

Another service locomotive to retain its London & North Western number, if not its number plate, was 0-6-0T No. 3323 used as a Crewe Works shunter. This much sought after veteran of the LNWR survived on internal duties at Crewe Works until 1954.

British Railways Standard Britannia Pacific No. 70046 "Anzac" at Sutton Coldfield in 1962 during it's brief sojourn at Aston depot. Shortly after this picture was taken, the engine returned to it's former home depot at Holyhead. "Anzac" was withdrawn in July 1967 and broken up by Campbell's at Airdrie in January 1968.

Arthur Mace remained active photographing steam until its final demise in 1968. During steam's final years he was resident in Birmingham and did many scenes in the area like this study of Black 5 No. 45058 in begrimed condition ekeing out its final days.

Ivatt Mogul 2-6-0, No. 46492 was one of a class of 128 engines built between 1946 and 1952. These useful light, mixed traffic engines then formed the basis for British Railways Standard 78000 Class.

A traditional line-up amid the interior of the Midland Railway roundhouse at Saltley, Birmingham with Class 3F 0-6-0s, 43435, 43674, 43680, 43620 and Class 4F 0-6-0, 43949.

Rendered surplus on the LT&SR lines by Stanier 3 cylinder 2-6-4Ts, this "Intermediate" Tilbury 4-4-2T of Class 2P No. 2104 has found its way to Mansfield for use on Nottingham trains. Other Tilbury 4-4-2s gravitated to Toton, Leicester and Skipton and the four examples from this last mentioned location ended their days rotting at Carlisle Durran Hill.

Ex-L&YR 4-6-0 No. 10415 in London & North Western livery stands at the buffer stops at Liverpool Exchange. Note the sign directing passengers to race trains for Aintree.

The sign
of good bread

A line-up of preserved engines in the paint shop at Crewe Works. From left to right, LNWR 2-4-0 No. 790 "Hardwicke"; 2-2-2 No. 3020 "Cornwall"; the Furness Railway 0-4-0 "Coppernob"; the replica of Stephenson's "Rocket" and 18 inch gauge 0-4-0T "Pet". Both Crewe and Horwich Works had extensive 18 inch gauge internal systems on which similar engines were employed for moving components and materials around the works site.

Over Page
With steam drifting helpfully for Arthur Mace, Stanier 8F 2-8-0 No. 48295 heads an up-freight through Stafford. The train spotters perched on top of the wall complete this early 1950's scene when steam trains were going to last forever.

Ex-MR Class 3F Jinty 0-6-0T No. 47249 undergoing a general overhaul in Derby Works in early BR days.

Possibly on the same visit to Derby Works, Arthur Mace found the cylinders of a Midland Compound 4-4-0. The low pressure ones with a diameter of 21 inches are placed at either side whilst the high pressure one of 19 inches diameter is at the centre.

THE PRINCESS ROYAL
6200

2
6200
3
4
SMETCHLEY
DRY CLEANING
KARRIER
HULL

Two unidentified Prince of Wales Class 4-6-0s. The leading engine is one of five fitted with Walschaerts valve gear in 1923/4. This picture is taken from one of Arthur Mace's 35mm negatives, a format he partially adopted in the post war years. The definition compares well with the much larger formats and glass plates of his pre-war work.

Over page
The first LMS Stanier Pacific No. 6200 "The Princess Royal" stands at Euston, a brand new engine in 1933. The Camden shed code 1 was changed to 1B in 1935. The original flat sided tender as applied to the first two members of this class looks incongruous and was soon replaced with the later standard variety.

Hughes "Crab" 2-6-0s were seldom seen working passenger trains on the southern reaches of the Midland Main Line. Occasionally however, they would turn up on specials like this one heading southwards through Market Harborough.

The magic that was once Warrington Bank Quay Station; a Patriot 4-6-0 heads an up express; a Stanier Class 8F 2-8-0 awaits the road whilst Ivatt 2-6-2T No. 41211 performs on the Earlestown push and pull train.

With the banking engine already attached, a Jubilee Class 4-6-0 takes water prior to ascending the Lickey Incline, meanwhile a Great Western Hall Class 4-6-0 waits with a freight train.

Previous page

Royal Scot Class 4-6-0 No. 46168 "The Girl Guide" surmounts the summit of the Lickey Incline at Blackwell with a lightweight three coach stopping passenger train. The Lickey Incline is Britain's steepest main line gradient.

27
SWITCH

Ex-London & North Western 0-8-0 No. 8942 freshly out-shopped from Crewe works after a major overhaul, is "run in" on light duty. Despite the introduction of some 700 Stanier 8Fs, these classic London & North Western heavy haulers remained ubiquitous well into the 1950's.

This incident at Stafford would have appealed to Arthur Mace's sense of humour. It shows LMS Class 3F Jinty 0-6-0T No. 47649 which has got itself into trouble while shunting a ventilated fruit van.

Ex-Midland Railway Class 4F 0-6-0 No. 43940 heads a southbound freight at Evesham. The former Great Western station can just be glimpsed on the far right.

46757

W730
3C

Former London & North Western Prince of Wales Class 4-6-0 No. 25704 "Scotia" heads a stopping passenger train.

Previous spread
Still in Midland Railway livery, Deeley 0-6-4T No. 2004 acts as Derby Station pilot with the works in the background. Known as Flatirons these engines were intended to replace Johnson's 0-4-4Ts on passenger work, but due to a tendency to derail they were confined to freight working. One of the Midland Railway's few unhappy designs, all had disappeared by 1938.

Over page
Ex-LNWR 2-4-2 No. 46757 is seen here in charge of a Stephenson Locomotive Society special which ran over closed branches in the Birmingham area on 3rd June in 1950. Based at Walsall, this 1897 built veteran survived until 1953. One hundred and sixty of these engines were built during the 1890s for branch and cross country work on the former London & North Western system; all had gone by 1955.

This is one of Arthur Mace's finest pictures and shows an unidentified rebuilt Claughton 4-6-0 heading a mixed freight. Believed to be a pre-war scene, the engine is possibly the last survivor No. 6004 (formally Princess Louise). The once 130 strong Claughton Class was an epic design in locomotive history and when No. 6004 was withdrawn in 1949 the London & North Western express passenger dynasty passed to extinction.

An ex-London & North Western Precursor 4-4-0 carries out a strange shunting movement in North Wales.

L M S
L M S
2004

40634
82
G

Ex-LNWR 0-6-2T Coal Tank No. 58900 (formally LMS 7699). This well known engine brought a latter day touch of North Western styling to Birmingham New Street where it ended its days as station pilot during the early 1950s working from Monument Lane shed. It was finally withdrawn in 1954.

Opposite
Ex-S&DJR Class 2P 4-4-0, No. 40634 stands at the buffer stops at Bath Green Park having assisted a BR Class 9F 2-10-0 over the Mendip Hills from Evercreech Junction with an express from Bournemouth West to the north.

This wonderful picture was one of Arthur Mace's favourites. He called it "A Crimson Rambler on it's native heath". Taken at 11am on a sunny July day in 1928, it shows a Midland Compound piloting a Deeley Belpaire 4-4-0 at Derby, the Midland Railway's spiritual home. In the background is a London and North Western Prince of Wales 4-6-0 on a Nottingham to Llandudno express.

Arthur Mace regularly visited Euston Station over a 35 year period and made a series of pictures of trains at the buffer stops. This scene, taken shortly after the grouping, shows a London and North Western Jumbo 2-4-0 acting as pilot to a Prince of Wales Class 4-6-0.

Several London and North Western Railway Claughton 4-6-0s were modified for the Midland Division loading gauge. No. 6005 is seen coupled to a tender from a Great Central design R.O.D. 2-8-0. This engine was replaced in 1932 by a Patriot Class 4-6-0 which eventually became No. 5509. On the left is 1867 built Midland Railway 2-4-0 No. 8, which survived until 1942.

Hughes Crab 2-6-0 No. 42886 and Stanier Class 5, 4-6-0 No. 44747 stand at Manchester Victoria.

Ex-LNWR George V Class 4-4-0 No. 25348 "Coronation" at speed with express passenger headlights. "Coronation" was the 5,000th engine built at Crewe works. She was withdrawn in 1940 after a working life of only 29 years. A preservation attempt was made and the engine languished in store for some years before tragically being broken up. The engine's name was duplicated in 1938 by the first of Stanier's Coronation Pacific's.

Previous spread
Webb built eight 0-4-2ST Crane Engines between 1892 and 1895 for duties at Crewe and Wolverton works. As service locomotives they retained their LNWR numbers in LMS days. No.3249, seen here at Crewe freshly out-shopped, was one of the last two survivors being withdrawn in 1947.

Introduction

The L.M.S. was the largest of the Big Four companies with territory ranging from Bristol to the Highlands of Scotland. Over ten thousand locomotives were inherited in 1923 from some of the largest railway companies in Britain such as the London and North Western, The Midland and the Caledonian. The L.M.S. was a rich potpourri of locomotive design and an extremely innovative railway especially during the tenancy of William Stanier who was Chief Mechanical Engineer from 1932 to 1944.

The Stanier years were one of the most productive periods in British railway history and produced a magnificent range of designs which revolutionised the L.M.S.'s motive power. The 8F 2-8-0 and Black Five 4-6-0s which together totalled over 1,700 engines, rapidly heralded the withdrawal of dozens of outmoded classes. Designs by Stanier and his successors Charles Fairburn and H.G. Ivatt, formed the basis for some of British Railways' standard designs built from 1951 onwards. When the L.M.S. passed into British Railways in 1948, it possesed 7,850 locomotives embracing 100 different designs.

Former LMS compound No. 41162 was a Rugby based engine. She was built by the Vulcan Foundry in 1925 and was one of the last survivors of the Compound 4-4-0 s. She was withdrawn in 1960 and the class became extinct the following year.

The Golden Years of British Steam Trains

LMS

LONDON MIDLAND & SCOTTISH RAILWAY

MILEPOST

A Class 1400 0-4-2T propels a B.R. built railmotor trailer on the approach to Hightown with a Wrexham to Ellesmere service.

Another push and pull train, probably on a Stourbridge service, with a Class 6400, 0-6-0PT in charge. The railmotor trailers are of G.W.R. and B.R. design respectively whilst behind the engine is a former L.M.S. van and a covered goods wagon.

At Birmingham Snow Hill, No.5955 "Garth Hall" of Didcot pauses with a down stopping train.

Previous spread
Crossing the River Dee at Chester, Class 5700 0-6-0PT No. 8730 heads an empty wagon train towards Saltney. These humble engines constituted Britain's largest class totalling 863 engines built between 1929 and 1949.

Appropriately named Hawksworth 4-6-0 No. 1006 "County of Cornwall" stands in Penzance Station with an up express.

Castle Class 4-6-0 No.5089 "Westminster Abbey" pauses in Bristol Temple Meads with the up Cornishman 10.30 am Penzance to Wolverhampton. Note the bevy of train spotters immersed in their task.

9
8730

Castle Class 4-6-0 No. 7031 "Cromwell's Castle" stands on the down relief line at Reading General at the head of a down Worcester express.

Previous spread
Another golden moment from the football specials on 27th April 1963 when the semi final of the F.A. cup was played at Aston Villa's ground bringing 15 special trains from the Southampton area into Birmingham Snow Hill. Here, entering Snow Hill's up platform is Stanier 8F No. 48417 piloting No. 34039 "Boscastle" on the 07.43 a.m. from Southampton. In the down platform stands No. 34094, one of only two un-rebuilt Bullied Pacifics used on these specials.

At Paddington, Oxford's No. 4979 "Wooton Hall" provides unusual motive power for the down Cathedrals Express normally worked by a Worcester Castle.

No. 6853 "Morehampton Grange" stands on an up express in the up loop platform at Birmingham's Snow Hill.

SUBWAY
REFRESHMENTS
LADIES
WAITING ROOM
7
PULLMAN
CAR
B
48417
DOWN
PULLMAN
CAR
A

5
GENTLEMEN
1270

Aberdare Class 2-6-0 No. 2676 running light near Oxford in 1935. These classic Dean engines were introduced in 1900 initially for work around the South Wales coalfields, hence their name. The type was given an extended life owing to World War Two and No. 2676 was not withdrawn until 1946; the last survivor following three years later

An Oswestry based Dean goods 0-6-0 No. 2424, heads a stopping passenger train. This engine escaped military service and was withdrawn in 1946.

The famous Bulldogs were introduced in 1898. They had a wonderful variety of names ranging from places in the British Empire, birds, notable rivers and famous celebrities. Most of the nameplates were of the traditional crescent design fitted to the forward wheel splashers but the example seen here is one of a few provided with oval cabside plates bearing both the name and the engine's number. The engine is No. 3327 ."Marco Polo" caught at Chester in April 1935 and withdrawn the following year. No. 3327 was one of the Bulldogs with curved frames; straight frames were introduced on the class commencing with No. 3341 in 1900.

Castle Class 4-6-0 No. 4078 "Pembroke Castle" in the up centre road at Bristol Temple Meads with two coaches to be added to the formation of an up Weston Super Mare express.

At the buffer stops at platform 1 Paddington where Hawksworth 0-6-0PT No. 9415 has brought in the empty coaches for the 11.30 a.m. Penzance departure. These were one of the last Great Western designs to be built; they were ordered at the end of 1947, immediately before nationalisation, and building continued into the early 1950's.

Castle Class 4-6-0 No.5046 "Earl Cawdor" - a Wolverhampton Stafford Road engine - has arrived at Shrewsbury

Dukedog 4-4-0 No. 9017 and a highly polished Manor 4-6-0 stand in Shrewsbury Station having been rostered to work the Cambrian Coast Express.

Three of the six 1934 built 1366 Class 0-6-0PT s in the stock shed at Swindon. Their main use was shunting those sidings in the works that required short wheel base engines and also on the Weymouth Harbour Tramway. In their final years they replaced the veteran Beattie 2-4-0T s at Wadebridge for the line to Wenford Bridge.

At Towyn on the Cambrian Coast Line, the 2' 3" gauge Talyllyn Railway is within easy access of the G.W.R. station. Talyllyn Railway 0-4-0WT "Dolgoch" of 1866 vintage stands at the line's Abergnolwyn terminus.

This delightful veteran was built by Sharp Stewart of Manchester in 1866. Numbered 1197, she was one of three 2-4-0Ts constructed for the Cambrian Railways and is seen in Oswestry Shed. She survived until 1948.

Un-rebuilt Bulleid Pacific No. 34094 "Mortehoe" enters Birmingham Snow Hill with the 08.00 a.m. special from Southampton Central.

On 27th April 1963 the semi-final of the F.A. cup was played at Aston Villa's ground. It brought 15 special trains from the Southampton area to Birmingham Snow Hill, all but one being hauled by Bulleid light Pacific's. Three of the football specials went via Worcester and were piloted by Class 8F 2-8-0's from Stourbridge. One of these, No. 48478, has assisted No. 34009 "Lyme Regis" on the 07.10 a.m. from Southampton. As the supporters leave Snow Hill Station the fireman stands in the Pacific's tender shovelling coal forward.

It's thumbs up from the train spotters eagerly awaiting the specials as No. 34088 "213 Squadron" heads the 08.49a.m. from Southampton Central into Birmingham Snow Hill.

WAY OUT AND
1, 2 & 3
7

The happy days of the School Treat are beautifully captured here by Arthur Mace. Invariably the excursions would be by train and performing the honours on this occasion is an 0-6-0PT.

Previous spread

Birmingham Snow Hill was one of Britain's best loved stations. It's architecture, it's light and shade effects, it's bustling atmosphere and glorious diversity of trains endeared it to the nation. Much of the magic is caught here as a King Class 4-6-0 arrives on a Birkenhead to Paddington express.

Class 14XX, 0-4-2T No. 1401 stands in the bay of the decrepit looking Banbury Station which was to be re-built in B.R. days. No. 1401 was in charge of a push and pull train to Chipping Norton and Kingham.

Another Class 14XX, 0-4-2T No. 1424 stands in Gloucester station with a Chalfont train. This service ceased at the end of 1964 and was the last push and pull working on former G.W.R. lines.

REFRESHMENTS
GENTLEMEN
A

WAY OUT
SUBWAY
REFRESHMENTS
5
THE FRENCH VIEW
HOME
WYMANS
LEFT LUGGAGE
TELEGRAMS

Ex-M.&S.W.J.R. 2-4-0 No. 1334 at Didcot on 11th May 1936. No. 1334 was one of three engines built by Dubs & Co. in 1894 and fitted with a G.W.R. standard boiler in 1924. These engines were used on the branch from Newbury to Lambourne.

Another double framed 0-6-0PT No. 1565 at Didcot, also on 11th May 1936. This example is fitted with a spark arresting chimney for working in local military stores depots. It survived until 1938.

The Dukedogs were a hybrid of Duke type boilers on Bulldog frames. These lively 4-4-0 s were light enough to work on lines such as those in the Cambrian section over which many larger engines were forbidden. No. 3212 "Earl of Eldon" is seen new at Swindon in May 1937. This engine was only named for a few weeks as its nameplates were transferred to the Castle Class 4-6-0 No. 5055 in July 1937.

0-6-0ST No. 1331 was a former Whitland and Cardigan Railway engine taken over by the Great Western in 1886. Built by Fox Walker & Co. in 1877, it was re-built at Swindon in 1927 and after a spell working on the Weymouth Harbour Tramway, it was transferred to Oswestry where this picture was made. The veteran was finally withdrawn in 1950.

1076 Class double framed 0-6-0PT No. 1574 was built as an 0-6-0ST in 1879 and rebuilt to the form seen here in 1927. Caught shunting at Oxford, No. 1574 was one of the last survivors of this large class and remained in service until 1937. Note the typical G.W.R. shunter's truck.

0-6-0PT No. 9700 was the first of eleven pannier tanks to be fitted with condensing gear for working over Metropolitan Railway sub-surface lines to the G.W.R. depot at Smithfield. The engine is seen at Old Oak Common Shed.

Cathedrals Express
A22

A double chimneyed Castle Class 4-6-0 on arrival at Paddington with the tightly timed Bristolian express. During the summer of 1959 this train was scheduled to cover the 118 miles between Paddington and Bristol in 100 minutes.

Opposite page
Another double chimneyed Castle at Worcester Shrub Hill on the up Cathedrals Express to Paddington.

Castle Class 4-6-0 No. 4095 "Harlech Castle" of Plymouth Laira Shed, stands in Bristol Temple Meads Station with an up empty stock train.

Churchward Class 43XX, 2-6-0 No. 7305 of Banbury Shed, stands at Leamington Spa General on a down stopping passenger train in August 1960. The camera wielding enthusiast seems totally absorbed in the proceedings.

One of the popular Saint Class 4-6-0's No. 2924 "St. Helena" enters Exeter St. David's with a north to west express, the formation including two ex-L.N.W.R. carriages. Built in 1907, No. 2924 lasted until 1950.

Duke Class 4-4-0 No. 3252 "Duke of Cornwall" stands in Shrewsbury Station in April 1935. Built in 1895 it was withdrawn in 1937 being replaced by a Dukedog 4-4-0.

V80